THE
POLITE LADIES'
GUIDE TO
PROPER ETIQUETTE

THE POLITE LADIES' GUIDE TO PROPER ETIQUETTE

A Complete Guide for a Lady's Conduct in All Her Relations Towards Society

ARTHUR MARTINE

Skyhorse Publishing

Skyhorse Publishing books may be purchased in bulk at special discounts for sales promotion, corporate gifts, fund-raising, or educational purposes. Special editions can also be created to specifications. For details, contact the Special Sales Department, Skyhorse Publishing, 307 West 36th Street, 11th Floor, New York, NY 10018 or info@skyhorsepublishing.com.

Skyhorse® and Skyhorse Publishing® are registered trademarks of Skyhorse Publishing, Inc.®, a Delaware corporation.

Visit our website at www.skyhorsepublishing.com.

10 9 8 7 6 5 4 3 2 1

Library of Congress Cataloging-in-Publication Data is available on file.

Cover design by Anthony Morais

Print ISBN: 978-1-63220-529-2
Ebook ISBN: 978-1-63220-904-7

Printed in the United States of America

CONTENTS

GENERAL OBSERVATIONS

POLITENESS has been defined as an "artificial good-nature," but it would be better said that *good-nature is natural politeness.* It inspires us with an unremitting attention, both to please others and to avoid giving them offense. Its code is a ceremonial, agreed upon and established among mankind, to give each other external testimonies of friendship or respect. *Politeness* and *etiquette* form a sort of supplement to the law, which enables society to protect itself against offences which the *law* cannot touch. For instance, the law cannot punish a man for habitually staring at people in an insolent and annoying manner, but *etiquette* can banish such an offender from the circles of good society, and fix upon him the brand of vulgarity. *Etiquette* consists in certain forms, ceremonies, and rules which the *principle of politeness* establishes and enforces for the regulation of the manners of men and women in their intercourse with each other.

Many unthinking persons consider the observance of etiquette to be nonsensical and unfriendly, as consisting of unmeaning forms, practiced only by the *silly* and the idle; an opinion which arises from their not having reflected on the *reasons* that have led to the establishment of certain rules indispensable to the well-being of society, and without which, indeed, it would inevitably fall to pieces, and be destroyed.

The true aim of politeness is to make those with whom you associate as well satisfied with themselves as possible. It does not, by any means, encourage an impudent self-importance in them, but it does whatever it can to accommodate their feelings and wishes in social intercourse. Politeness is a sort of social benevolence, which avoids wounding the pride, or shocking the prejudices of those around you.

The principle of politeness is the same among all nations, but the ceremonials which etiquette imposes differ according to the taste and habits of various countries. For instance, many of the minor rules of etiquette at Paris differ from those at London; and at New York they may differ from both Paris and London. But still the polite of every country have about the same manners.

Of the manners and deportment of both ladies and gentlemen, we would remark that a proper consideration for the welfare and comfort of others will generally lead to a greater propriety of demeanor than any rules which the most rigid master of etiquette could supply. This feeling, however, is one that must be cultivated, for the promptings of nature are eminently selfish, and courtesy and good-breeding are only attainable by effort and discipline. But even courtesy has limits where dignity should govern it, for when carried to excess, particularly in manner, it borders on sycophancy, which is almost as despicable as rudeness. To overburden people with attention; to render them uncomfortable with a prodigality of proffered services; to insist upon obligations which they do not desire, is not only to render yourself disagreeable, but contemptible. This defect of manners is particularly prevalent in the rural districts, where the intense effort to render a visitor comfortable has exactly the contrary effect; besides, there are those whose want of refinement and good breeding often leads them to an unwarrantable familiarity, which requires coldness and indifference to subdue.

Much misconstruction and unpleasant feeling arises, especially in country towns, from not knowing what is *"expected"* or necessary to be done on certain occasions; resulting sometimes from the prevalence of local customs, with which the world in general are not supposed to be acquainted. "To do in Rome as the Romans do," applies to every kind of society. At the same time, you can never be expected to commit a serious breach of manners because your neighbors do so.

But what you should do, and what not, in particular cases, you will learn in the following chapters. I have only now to say, that if you wish to be agreeable, which is certainly a good and religious desire, you must both study how to be so, and take the trouble to put your studies into constant practice. The fruit you will soon reap. You will be generally liked and loved. The gratitude of those to whom you have devoted yourself will be shown in speaking well of you; you will become a desirable addition to every party, and whatever your birth, fortune, or position, people will say of you, "He is a most agreeable and well-bred man," and be glad to introduce you to good society. But you will reap a yet better reward. You will have in yourself the satisfaction of having taken trouble and made sacrifices in order to give pleasure and happiness for the time to others. How do you know what grief or care you may not obliterate, what humiliation you may not alter to confidence, what anxiety you may not soften, what—last, but really not least—what intense dullness you may not enliven? If this work assist you in becoming an agreeable member of good society, I shall rejoice at the labor it has given me.

THE ART OF CONVERSATION

As the object of conversation is pleasure and improvement, those subjects only which are of universal interest can be made legitimate topics of pleasantry or discussion. And it is the gift of expressing thoughts and fancies in a quick, brilliant, and graceful manner on such topics—of striking out new ideas, eliciting the views and opinions of others, of attaching the interest of all to the subject discussed, giving it, however trifling in itself, weight and importance in the estimation of the hearers, that constitutes the great talent for conversation. But this talent can never, we may safely aver, be displayed except in a good cause, and when conversation is carried on in a spirit of genuine charity and benevolence.

We should meet in society to please and be pleased, and not to display cold and stately dignity, which is as much out of place, as all attempts to shine by a skillful adherence to the fantastic rules of the silver-fork school, are puerile and ludicrous. Such little things are great to little persons, who are proud of having acquired by rote, what the naturally elegant derive, in sufficient measure, from naturally just feeling.

The power of preserving silence is the very first requisite to all who wish to shine, or even please in discourse; and those who cannot preserve it, have really no business to speak. Of course, I do not mean the dull, ignorant, sulky, or supercilious silence, of which we see enough in all conscience; but the graceful, winning, and eloquent silence. The silence that, without any deferential air, listens with polite attention, is more flattering than compliments, and more frequently broken for the purpose of encouraging others to speak, than to display the listener's own powers. This is the really eloquent silence. It requires great genius—more perhaps than speaking—and few are gifted with the talent; but it is of such essential advantage, that I must recommend its study to all who are desirous to take a share in conversation, and beg they will learn to be silent, before they attempt to speak.

Notwithstanding the praise here bestowed on silence, *it* must still be explained that there are various modes of being silently rude. There is the rude silence of disdain— of not hearing, of not even deeming your words deserving attention or reply. These are minor and mere passive modes of impertinence; the direct and active sort of silent rudeness is to listen with a fixed and attentive stare on the speaker, and without any necessity of raising the eyebrows—for that might be precarious—show your utter amazement, that anyone should think of thus addressing a person of your rank, wealth, genius, or greatness. There are of course various styles and degrees in all these, modes of impertinence, but they all originate in the same cause; ignorance of the real facility of being rude, and a wish to acquire distinction by the practice. It is idle to assert that every one can be rude if he likes; for, if such were the fact, we should not see hosts of persons belonging to what is termed good society, seeking fame and renown by various shades and degrees of mere impertinence.

Never give short or sharp answers in ordinary conversation, unless you aspire to gain distinction by mere rudeness; for they have in fact no merit, and are only uncivil. "I do not know," "I cannot tell," are the most harmless words possible, and may yet be rendered very offensive by the tone and manner in which they are pronounced. Never reply, in answer to a question like the following, "Did Mrs. Spitewell tell you how Miss Rosebud's marriage was getting on?" "I did not ask." It is almost like saying, I never ask impertinent questions, though you do; we learn plenty of things in the world without having first inquired about them. If you must say, you did not ask, say, that "you forgot to ask," "neglected it," or "did not think of it." We can always be ordinarily civil, even if we cannot always be absolutely wise.

Except in mere sport and raillery, and where a little *extravaganza* is the order of the moment, always when you answer, or speak in reply to an observation made, speak to the true and just import of what is said. Leave quibbling of every kind to lawyers pleading at the bar for the life of a culprit; in society and conversation it is invariably out of place, unless when Laughter is going his merry round. At all other times it is a proof of bad breeding.

You must not overstretch a proposition, neither must you overstretch or spin out a jest, that has done its duty; for few can be made to rebound after they have once come to the ground.

Another mode of being rude, is to collect, and have at command, all the set phrases used by uncivil persons, in order to say what they fancy very sharp and severe things. Such a collector, jealous perhaps of the attention with which a pleasant guest is listened to, may break in upon the most harmless discourse with the words, "I think you *lie* under a mistake." The term may in itself be harmless, but its application is at all times rude, coarse, and decidedly vulgar.

La Bruyère tells us that "rudeness is not a fixed and inherent vice of the mind, but the result of other vices; it springs," he says, "from vanity, ignorance, laziness, stupidity, jealousy, and inattention. It is the more hateful from being constantly displayed in exterior deportment, and from being thus always visible and manifest; and is offensive in character and degree according to the source from which it takes its rise."

We next come to the loud talker, the man who silences a whole party by his sole power of lungs. All subjects are alike to him; he speaks on every topic with equal fluency, is never at a loss, quotes high authority for every assertion, and allows no one else to utter a word; he silences, without the least ceremony, every attempt at interruption, however cleverly managed—calls out, "I beg your pardon," in a tone that shows how ill-used he thinks himself—or shuts your mouth with—"One minute, if you please, sir!" as much as to say, you are surely a very ill-bred fellow. Great, and especially loud and positive talkers, have been denounced by all writers on manners as shallow and superficial persons. And P. Andre, the author of a French Essay on the Beautiful, declares distinctly, that "no man of sense was ever a great talker."

Next to the talker, we have the man who gives an account of his dogs, horses, lands, books, and pictures. Whatever is his, must, he thinks, interest others; and listen they must, however resolutely they may attempt to change the current of his discourse.

Women of this class are sometimes too fond of praising their children. It is no doubt an amiable weakness; but I would still advise them to indulge as little as possible in the practice; for however dear the rosy-cheeked, curly-headed prattlers may be to them, the chances are, that others will vote the darlings to be great bores; you that have children, never speak of them in company. You must not even praise your near relations; for the subject deprives the hearer of all power to dissent, and is therefore clearly objectionable.

In the same line is the clever bore, who takes up every idle speech, to show his wisdom at a cheap rate. If you say, "Hang the weather!" before such a man, he immediately proves, by logical demonstrations, that the weather has no neck by which it can be suspended. The grave expounder of truisms belongs to this class. He cannot allow the simplest conversation to go on, without entering into proofs and details familiar to every child nine years of age; and the tenor of his discourse, however courteous in terms and manner, pays you the very indifferent compliment of supposing that you have fallen from some other planet, in total and absolute ignorance of the most ordinary and every-day things connected with this little world of ours. All foreigners are particularly great at this style of boring.

Then you have the indifferent and apathetic bore, who hardly condescends to pay the least attention to what you say; and who, if he refrains from the direct and absolute rudeness of yawning in your face, shows, by short and drawling answers, given at fits and starts, and completely at variance with the object of the conversation, that he affects at least a total indifference to the party present, and to the subject of discourse. In society, the absent man is uncivil; he who affects to be so, is rude and vulgar. All persons who speak of their ailings, diseases, or bodily infirmities, are offensive bores. Subjects of this sort should be addressed to doctors, who are paid for listening to them, and to no one else. Bad taste is the failing of these bores. Then we have the ladies and gentlemen who pay long visits, and who, meeting you at the door prepared to sally forth, keep you talking near the fire till the beauty of the day is passed; and then take their leave, "hoping they have not detained you." Bad feeling or want of tact here predominates.

"Hobby-riders," who constantly speak on the same eternal subject—who bore you at all times and at all hours—whether you are in health or in sickness, in spirits or in sorrow, with the same endless topic, must not be over-looked in our list; though it is sufficient to denounce them. Their failing is occasioned by a total want of judgment.

The *Malaprops* are also a numerous and unhappy family, for they are constantly addressing the most unsuitable speeches to individuals or parties. To the blind they will speak of fine pictures and scenery; and will entertain a person in deep mourning with the anticipated pleasures of tomorrow's ball. A total want of ordinary thought and observation, is the general cause of the *Malaprop* failing.

Let us add to this very imperfect list the picture of a bore described by Swift. "Nothing," he says, "is more generally exploded than the folly of talking too much; yet I rarely remember to have seen five people together, where Someone among them hath not been predominant in that kind, to the great constraint and disgust of all the rest. But among such as deal in multitudes of words, none are comparable to the sober, deliberate talker, who proceedeth with much thought and caution, maketh his preface, brancheth out into several digressions, findeth a hint that putteth him in mind of another story, which he promises to tell you when this is done, cometh back regularly to his subject, cannot readily call to mind some person's name, holdeth his head, complaineth of his memory; the whole company all this while in suspense; at last says, it is no matter, and so goes on. And to crown the business, it perhaps proveth at last a story the company has heard heard fifty times before, or at best some insipid adventure of the relater."

To this we may add, that your cool, steady talkers, who speak with the care and attention of professors demonstrating mathematical problems—who weigh, measure and balance every word they utter—are all decided objectionables in society. It is needless to say, that such persons never blunder, and never "stumble over a potato;" a matter of little recommendation. In conversation there must be, as in love and in war, some hazarding, some rattling on; nor need twenty falls affect you, so long as you take cheerfulness and good humor for your guides; but the careful and measured conversation just described is always, though perfectly correct, extremely dull and tedious—a vast blunder from first to last.

There are also many persons who commence speaking before they know what they are going to say. The ill-natured world, who never miss an opportunity of being severe, declare them to be foolish and destitute of brains. I shall not go so far; but hardly know what we should think of a sportsman who would attempt to bring down a bird before he had loaded his gun.

I have purposely reserved the egotistical bore for the last on this short and imperfect list. It is truly revolting, indeed, to approach the very *Boa-constrictor* of good society; the snake who comes upon us, not in the natural form of a huge, coarse, slow reptile, but Proteus-like, in a thousand different forms; though all displaying at the first sight the boa-bore, ready to slime over every subject of discourse with the vile saliva of selfish vanity. Pah! it is repulsive even to speak of the species, numerous, too, as the sands along the shore.

Some of the class make no ceremony of immediately intruding themselves and their affairs on the attention of a whole party; of silencing every other subject started, however interesting to the company, merely that they may occupy the prominent and most conspicuous position. Others again are more dexterous, and with great art will lie on the watch to hook in their own praise. They will call a witness to remember they always foretold what would happen in such a case, but none would believe them; they advised such a man from the beginning, and told him the consequences just as they happened; but he would have his own way. Others make a vanity of telling their own faults; they are the strangest men in the world; they cannot dissemble; they own it is a folly; they have lost abundance of advantages by it; but if you would give them the world, they cannot help it; there is something in their nature that abhors insincerity and constraint, with many other insufferable topics of the same altitude. Thus, though bores find their account in speaking ill or well of themselves, it is the characteristic of a gentleman that he never speaks of himself at all.

La Bruyère says, "The great charm of conversation consists less in the display of one's own wit and intelligence, than in the power to draw forth the resources of others; he who leaves you after a long conversation, pleased with himself and the part *he* has taken in the discourse, will be your warmest admirer. Men do not care to admire you, they wish you to be pleased with them; they do not seek for instruction or even amusement from your discourse, but they do wish you to be made acquainted with their talents and powers of conversation; and the true man of genius will delicately make all who come in contact with him feel the exquisite satisfaction of knowing that they have appeared to advantage."

I have no desire to condemn my readers to eternal silence; but must inform them that it is not so easy to *shine* in conversation as many suppose. Fluency of tongue and a little modest assurance, though very well for imposing on the unwary, go but a short way when you have to deal with those who are really worth pleasing.

How can a person *shine* by conversation in elegant and educated society, whose thoughts have never ranged beyond the gratification of foolish vanity and mean selfishness; who has never reflected on life, men, and manners; whose mind has not turned to the contemplation of the works and wonders of nature; and who, in the events of his own time, has not seen the results of the many deeds of sorrow, shame, greatness, and glory, that crowd the pages of the world's variegated annals? Whoever would *shine* in polite discourse must at least be well versed in the philosophy of life, and possess a fair acquaintance with, general and natural history, and the outlines of science. And though he need be neither a poet nor an artist, he must be well read in poetry and acquainted with fine arts; because it is only by their study that taste can be cultivated and fancy guided. A familiarity with the fine arts is necessary, in fact, to give him a just perception of the sublime and beautiful, the very foundation whence our emotions of delight must arise. Anyone attempting to *shine* in conversation, without possessing the trifling acquirements here mentioned— for I have said nothing of learning and science—will most assuredly make an indifferent figure, and had better therefore content himself with simply pleasing by unaffected cheerfulness and good humor, which is within reach of all.

As to subjects for conversation, what difficulty can there be about them? Will not books, balls, bonnets and metaphysics furnish pleasant topics of discourse? Can you not speak of the

> Philosophy and science, and the springs
> Of wonder, and the wisdom of the world?

Are flirtations, traveling, love, and speech-making at an end; or is the great globe itself and the weather on its surface so perfectly stationary that you can find nothing to say about them? No, no, let us not deceive ourselves; we never want subjects of conversation; but we often want the knowledge how to treat them; above all, how to bring them forward in a graceful and pleasing manner. We often want observation and a just estimate of character, and do not know how, in the present defective state of society, any passing remark intended to open a conversation may be received.

Cheerfulness, unaffected cheerfulness, a sincere desire to please and be pleased, unchecked by any efforts to shine, are the qualities you must bring with you into society, if you wish to succeed in conversation. Under the influence of their recommendation, you may safely give the rein to fancy and hilarity, certain that, in a well-assorted party, you will make at least a favorable impression, if not a brilliant one. I do not of course mean by cheerfulness any outbreaking of loud and silly mirth, nor what the world sometimes calls a "high flow of spirits," but a light and airy equanimity of temper—that spirit which never rises to boisterousness, and never sinks to immovable dullness; that moves gracefully "from grave to gay, from serious to serene," and by mere manner gives proof of a feeling heart and generous mind.

Franklin says, that you must never contradict in conversation, nor correct facts if wrongly stated. This is going much too far; you must never contradict in a short, direct, or positive tone; but with politeness, you may easily, when necessary, express a difference of opinion in a graceful and even complimentary manner. And I would almost say, that the art of conversation consists in knowing *how* to contradict, and *when* to be silent; for, as to constantly acting a fawning and meanly deferential part in society, it is offensive to all persons of good sense and good feeling. In regard to facts wrongly stated, no well-bred man ever thinks of correcting them, merely to show his wisdom in trifles; but with politeness, it is perfectly easy to rectify an error, when the nature of the conversation demands the explanation.

Whenever the lady or gentleman with whom you are discussing a point, whether of love, war, science or politics, begins to sophisticate, drop the subject instantly. Your adversary either wants the ability to maintain his opinion—and then it would be uncivil to press it—or he wants the still more useful ability to yield the point with unaffected grace and good-humor; or what is also possible, his vanity is in some way engaged in defending views on which he may probably have acted, so that to demolish his opinions is perhaps to reprove his conduct, and no well-bred man goes into society for the purpose of sermonizing.

All local wits, all those whose jests are understood only within the range of their own circle or coterie, are decided objectionables in general society. It is the height of ill-breeding, in fact, to converse, or jest, on subjects that are not perfectly understood by the party at large; it is a species of rude mystification, as uncivil as whispering, or as speaking in language that may not be familiar to some of the party. But you must not make a fool of yourself, even if others show themselves deficient in good manners; and must not, like inflated simpletons, fancy yourself the object of every idle jest you do not understand, or of every laugh that chance may have called forth. *Ladies and gentlemen* feel that they are neither laughed at nor ridiculed.

In society, the object of conversation is of course entertainment and improvement, and it must, therefore, be adapted to the circle in which it is carried on, and must be neither too high nor too deep for the party at large, so that every one may contribute his share, just at his pleasure, and to the best of his ability. Let no two or three old Indians, old school-fellows, or old brother campaigners, seize upon the conversation to themselves, discuss their former adventures, and keep the rest of a party listening silently to an animated conversation about exploded stories, of which they know nothing and care as little.

Lord Chesterfield advises his son "to speak often, but not to speak much at a time; so that if he does not please, he will not at least displease to any great extent." A good observer should easily, I think, be able to discover whether he pleases or not.

Rousseau tells us, that "persons who know little talk a great deal, while those who know a great deal say very little."

If the discourse is of a grave or serious nature, and interesting to the party, or to any number of the party, never break in upon it with any display of idle wit or levity; for nothing shows so great a want of good manners; nor must you ever ridicule or doubt the existence of any noble enthusiasm that may have called forth expressions of admiration; for there is no want of high worth, patriotism, honor, and disinterestedness on earth. Your incredulity might therefore be unjust, and it is at all times a proof of bad taste to ridicule what others admire.

If you join in the graver conversation, intended to move the deeper feelings of the heart, do so without affectation, without overstretching sentiments, or bringing in farfetched ideas for the sake of producing effect, otherwise you will be sure to fail. Avoid, above all, when on such topics, any stringing together of unmeaning words; for bad as the practice of substituting sound for sense is at all times, it is doubly so when conversation takes the direction of which we are speaking, as it then shows the *jingler* to want feelings as well as ideas. Speak from the heart, when you speak *to* the heart; only making judgment prune the expressions of deep feeling, without checking the noble sentiments that may have called them forth.

The reason which renders this pruning system advisable is that society swarms with worthy, respectable persons, possessing an ordinary share of superficial good-nature, but so destitute of actual feeling, as not even to understand its language; and who, without being scoffers, will be inclined to laugh at expressions that convey no ideas to their minds.

The same reason should serve as a warning to all gentlemen against writing love-letters; for if a gentle swain is really and truly in love, he will write under excited feelings; and a letter written with a palpitating heart, threatening to break a rib at every throb, can hardly fail to appear a little ridiculous in the eyes of all who may not chance to be exactly in the same frame of mind, or possessed of the same degree of feeling with the writer.

There is a giggling and laughing tone, in which ladies and gentlemen sometimes endeavor to speak— an attempt to continue a series of jests from the first to last, which is not only foolish, but actually offensive. Conversation can never be kept up to the laughing point during a whole evening—not even during a morning visit; and efforts to excite laughter by overstrained jests are as repulsive as overstrained efforts to groan and grimace it. The natural flow of discourse must be calm and serene; if wit, whim, fun, and fire are present, they will not fail to flash brightly along its surface; but they can never constitute the main body of the stream itself.

Different parties, different tones no doubt, and an assembly of grave doctors and professors, meeting to discuss some learned subject, may treat it in their own way; here we can only speak of general society. It is said, that the guests at a pleasant dinner party should never exceed the number of the Muses, nor fall below that of the Graces. And this may be true; but a party of three or four is already very different in character—independent of the difference occasioned by the characters of the guests—from what a party of eight or nine will be. In small parties of this kind, numbers alone exercise great influence. But large or small, always recollect that you can have no right to complain of the dullness of the conversation, unless you have contributed your best efforts to render it cheerful.

Nor is it always right to condemn a person for being silent in company, as this often results from the nature of the party, which may be ill-assorted, though composed of deserving people. No one can maintain a conversation by himself; the very best speaker must still be aided by others, who must lend assistance in the *proper spirit, befitting* the nature of the discourse; for a rude and forward person, wishing to shine, can easily crush the efforts of the most perfect gentleman, and give an unfavorable tone and turn to a pleasant conversation.

In ordinary conversation, the modulation and proper management of the voice is a point to which I would particularly call the attention of young ladies; for a fine and melodious voice, "sweet as music on the waters," makes the heart-strings vibrate to their very core. This can only be done by a certain degree of confidence, and by a total absence of affectation; for uncertainty, agitation, and striving for effect are always ruinous to the voice of the speaker, which is constantly running against breakers, or getting upon flats. I am certain that temper and disposition are far more generally, and more perfectly marked by the voice and manner of speaking, than we are at all willing to allow.

The thin, small voice is the most difficult to manage, as it is liable to degenerate into shrillness; and ladies who have this kind of voice must keep strict guard over their temper, when within hearing of anyone on whom they may wish to make a favorable impression; for the very idea of a shrill-voiced scold makes us place our hands to our ears. But with a sweet temper, a pretty, little, harmonious voice is pleasing enough. Always recollect, however, that affectation, constraint, or striving for effect, is the certain ruin of the prettiest voice in the world.

The very deep-toned voice, though extremely effective when well controlled, has great difficulties; for unless backed by kind, cheerful, and airy feeling, by "that bright spirit which is always gladness," it is liable to fall into a coarse, rude and vulgar tone, and should never be heard except at times of brilliant sunshine. The owners of such voices should never think of getting angry, nor even indulge in saying what they may fancy sharp or severe things, as the chances are, that they will prove only rude ones.

Stories, however good—and they are often to be recommended—suffer under one of the disadvantages to which anecdotes are liable—they do not bear repetition; and no one can be expected to possess a stock that shall furnish new and acceptable wares on every occasion. They form in conversation the resource of those who want imagination, and must be received with indulgence; but to deserve this favor, they must be short, well told, well pointed, and judiciously adapted to the feelings and composition of the party. We have all of us at times known a good story or anecdote introduced under such inappropriate circumstances, as to make a whole party look grave and feel uncomfortable.

The honor of demolishing the weavers of long tales shall be left to Cowper.

> But sedentary weavers of long tales
> Give me the fidgets, and my patience fails.
> 'Tis the most asinine employ on earth,
> To hear them tell of parentage and birth;
> And echo conversations dull and dry,
> Embellished with *he said* and *so said I.*
> At every interview their route the same,
> The repetition makes attention lame;
> We bristle up with unsuccessful speed,
> And in the saddest part, cry—*Droll, indeed.*

Let the reader only get these verses by heart, and repeat a line occasionally to show that he recollects them, and we shall soon find society relieved from these spinners of dull yarns.

Some gentlemen have a talent for placing things in a grotesque, exaggerated, and ludicrous light; and of extemporizing burlesque anecdotes in a whimsical and amusing manner. It is a happy gift, of which excellent use can be made in society; but tact and taste must, as usual, keep a firm rein, for nothing that is seriously treated by others must ever be burlesqued and turned into ridicule. The grotesque style is only applicable when the ground is fairly open, or when jesting, bantering, and exaggeration are the order of the minute; and then it may be rendered charming.

Let no one suppose that mimicry is to be sanctioned under this head; far from it, indeed. A little graceful imitation of actors and public speakers may be allowed. National manners, and the peculiarities of entire classes, are fair game. French dandies, Yankee bargainers, and English exquisites, may be ridiculed at pleasure; you may even bring forward Irish porters, cab-drivers and bog-trotters—*provided* you can imitate their wit and humor; but I do not think I ever saw any mimicry of private individuals well received by well-bred persons. Nor is this to be wondered at, since mimicry borders so closely on buffoonery, as generally to end in absolute vulgarity. Ladies, however, may be permitted to mimic their friends a little, provided they rarely indulge in the practice, and never transgress the bounds of good taste and elegance.

We meet occasionally in society with persons belonging to a class, not numerous indeed, but deserving notice, as they are mostly ladies, and often worth reclaiming; for want of a better term I shall call them *Icicles*, because they only shine and cannot warm. The *Icicles* may be kind, clever, of cultivated mind, and in every respect well disposed to become agreeable—but cannot speak or converse on anyone subject. They are constantly witty and ingenious, place every proposition or general question asked in some amusing, novel or extravagant light, but never answer or speak up to the point; so that you may converse with them for hours, and be acquainted with them for years, without knowing their opinion upon anyone subject; without knowing even whether they have an opinion on anyone subject. Nor does this always result from affectation, or from efforts to shine; it springs as often from a faulty tone, and the fear of not being sufficiently clever, when attempting to be rational, as from any other source.

I have seen persons lose a great deal by this absurd system, and fall far short of what they might have been had they merely followed the beaten track; and as a maxim would have you recollect, that few good things are ever said by those who are constantly striving to say extraordinary ones.

GENERAL RULES FOR CONVERSATION

As order or method are of very little consequence in treating of this subject, I will conclude by giving a series of rules upon the art of conversation, couched in a few words, from which the reader may furnish himself with a competent knowledge of what is to be studied, and what to be avoided. There are few of the following sentences that will not furnish a good deal of thought, or that are to be understood to their full extent without some consideration.

Whatever passes in parties at your own or another's house is never repeated by well-bred people. Things of no moment, and which are meant only as harmless jokes, are liable to produce unpleasant consequences if repeated. To repeat, therefore, any conversation which passes on such occasions, is understood to be a breach of confidence, which should banish the offender from the pale of good society.

Men of all sorts of occupations meet in society. As they go there to unbend their minds and escape from the fetters of business, you should never, in an evening, speak to a man about his profession. Do not talk of politics to a journalist, of fevers to a physician, of stocks to a broker—nor, unless you wish to enrage him to the utmost, of education to a collegian. The error which is here condemned is often committed from mere good nature and a desire to be affable. But it betrays to a gentleman, ignorance of the world—to a philosopher, ignorance of human nature.

A gentleman will, by all means, avoid showing his learning and accomplishments in the presence of ignorant and vulgar people, who can, by no possibility, understand or appreciate them. It is a pretty sure sign of bad breeding to set people to staring and feeling uncomfortable.

In England, it is regarded a breach of etiquette to repeat the name of any person with whom you are conversing. But the same rule does not hold in America. Here it is deemed no breach, if you are conversing with a lady by the name of Sherwood, to say, "Well, *Mrs. Sherwood*, do you not think," etc.

In a mixed company, never speak to your friend of a matter which the rest do not understand, unless it is something which you can explain to them, and which may be made interesting to the whole party.

If you wish to inquire about anything, do not do it by asking a question; but introduce the subject, and give the person an opportunity of saying as much as he finds it agreeable to impart. Do not even say, "How is your brother today?" but "I hope your brother is quite well."

Never ask a lady a question about anything whatever.

By all means, avoid the use of slang terms and phrases in polite company. No greater insult can be offered to polite society than to repeat the slang dictums of barrooms and other low places. If you are willing to have it known that you are familiar with such company yourself, you have no right to treat a party of ladies and gentlemen as though they were, too.

Avoid the habit of employing French words in English conversation; it is extremely bad taste to be always using such expressions as *ci-devant, soi-disant, en masse, couleur de rose,* etc. Do not salute your acquaintances with *bon jour,* nor reply to every proposition, *volontiers.* In society, avoid having those peculiar preferences for some subjects which are vulgarly denominated "*hobby-horses.*" They make your company a *bore* to all your friends; and some kind-hearted creature will take advantage of them and *trot* you, for the amusement of the company. Every attempt to obtrude on a company subjects either to which they are indifferent, or of which they are ignorant, is in bad taste.

Man should be taught as though you taught him not,
And things unknown proposed as things forgot.

A man is quite sure to show his good or bad breeding the instant he opens his mouth to talk in company. If he is *a gentleman* he starts no subject of conversation that can possibly be displeasing to any person present. The ground is common to all, and no one has a right to monopolize any part of it for his own particular opinions, in politics or religion. No one is there to make proselytes, but every one has been invited, to be *agreeable* and *to please.*

He who knows the world, will not be too bashful. He who knows himself, will not be impudent.

Do not endeavor to shine in all companies. Leave room for your hearers to imagine something within you beyond all you have said. And remember, the more you are praised, the more you will be envied.

There is no surer sign of vulgarity than the perpetual boasting of the fine things you have at home. If you speak of your silver, of your jewels, of your costly apparel, it will be taken for a sign that you are either lying, or that you were, not long ago, somebody's washerwoman, and cannot forget to be reminding everybody that you are not so now.

You need not tell all the truth, unless to those who have a right to know it all. But let all you tell be truth.

Insult not another for his want of a talent you possess; he may have others, which you want. Praise your friends and let your friends praise you.

If you treat your inferiors with familiarity, expect the same from them. If you give a jest, take one. Let all your jokes be truly jokes. Jesting sometimes ends in sad earnest.

If a favor is asked of you, grant it, if you can. If not, refuse it in such a manner, as that one denial may be sufficient.

If you are in company with a distinguished gentleman— as a governor, or senator—you will not be perpetually trying to trot out his titles, as it would make you appear like a lackey or parasite, who, conscious of no merits of your own, are trying to lift yourself by the company of others. In introducing such a gentleman, you will merely call him "governor," or "senator," and afterwards avoid all allusion to his rank.

If you would render yourself pleasing in social parties, never speak to gratify any particular vanity or passion of your own, but always aim to interest or amuse others by themes which you know are in accordance with their tastes and understandings. Even a well-bred minister will avoid introducing his professional habits and themes at such places. He knows that the guests were not invited there to listen to a sermon, and there may be some who differ with him in opinions, who would have good reason to feel themselves insulted by being thus forced to listen to him.

Reproof is a medicine like mercury or opium; if it be improperly administered, with report either to the adviser or the advised, it will do harm instead of good.

Nothing is more unmannerly than to reflect on any man's profession, sect, or natural infirmity. He who stirs up against himself another's self-love, provokes the strongest passions in human nature.

Be careful of your word, even in keeping the most trifling appointment. But do not blame another for a failure of that kind, till you have heard his excuse.

Never offer advice, but where there is some probability of its being followed.

If you find yourself in a company which violently abuses an absent friend of yours, you need not feel that you are called upon to take up the club for him. You will do better by saying mildly that they must have been misinformed—that you are proud to call him your friend, which you could not do if you did not know him to be incapable of such things as they had heard. After this, if they are gentlemen, they will stop—indeed, if they had been gentlemen, they would hardly have assailed an absent one in a mixed party; and if you feel constrained to quit their company, it will be no sacrifice to your own self-respect or honor.

Fools pretend to foretell what will be the issue of things, and are laughed at for their awkward conjectures. Wise men, being aware of the uncertainty of human affairs, and having observed how small a matter often produces a great change, are modest in their conjectures.

He who talks too fast, outruns his hearer's thoughts. He who speaks too slow, gives his hearer pain by hindering his thoughts, as a rider who frets his horse by reining him in too much.

Never think to entertain people with what lies out of their way, be it ever so curious in its kind. Who would think of regaling a circle of ladies with the beauties of Homer's Greek, or a mixed company with Sir Isaac Newton's discoveries?

Do well, but do not boast of it. For that will lessen the commendation you might otherwise have deserved.

Never ask a question under any circumstances. In the first place, it is too proud; in the second place, it may be very inconvenient or very awkward to give a reply. A lady inquired of what branch of medical practice a certain gentleman was professor. He held the chair of *midwifery*!

To offer advice to an angry man, is like blowing against a tempest.

Too much preciseness and solemnity in pronouncing what one says in common conversation, as if one was preaching, is generally taken for an indication of self-conceit and arrogance.

Make your company a rarity, and people will value it. Men despise what they can easily have.

Value truth, however you come by it. Who would not pick up a jewel that lay on a dung-hill?

The beauty of behavior consists in the manner, not the matter of your discourse.

It is not in good taste for a lady to say "Yes, sir," and "No, sir," to a gentleman, or frequently to introduce the word "Sir," at the end of her sentence, unless she desire to be exceedingly reserved toward the person with whom she is conversing.

If your superior treats you with familiarity, it will not therefore become you to treat him in the same manner.

A good way to avoid impertinent and pumping inquiries, is by answering with another question. An evasion may also serve the purpose. But a lie is inexcusable on any occasion, especially when used to conceal the truth from one who has no authority to demand it.

To reprove with success, the following circumstances are necessary, viz.: mildness, secrecy, intimacy, and the esteem of the person you would reprove.

If you be nettled with severe raillery, take care never to show that you are stung, unless you choose to provoke more. The way to avoid being made a butt, is not to set up for an archer.

To set up for a critic is bullying mankind.

Reflect upon the different appearances things make to you from what they did some years ago, and don't imagine that your opinion will never alter, because you are extremely positive at present. Let the remembrance of your past changes of sentiment make you more flexible.

If ever you were in a passion, did you not find reason afterwards to be sorry for it, and will you again allow yourself to be guilty of a weakness, which will certainly be in the same manner followed by repentance, besides being attended with pain?

Never argue with any but men of sense and temper.

It is ill-manners to trouble people with talking too much either of yourself, or your affairs. If you are full of yourself, consider that you, and your affairs, are not so interesting to other people as to you.

Keep silence sometimes, upon subjects which you are known to be a judge of. So your silence, where you are ignorant, will not discover you.

To use phrases which admit of a double meaning is un-gentlemanly, and, if addressed to a lady, they become positively insulting.

There is a vulgar custom, too prevalent, of calling almost everybody "colonel" in this country, of which it is sufficient to say, that this false use of titles prevails most among the lower ranks of society—a fact which sufficiently stamps upon it its real character, and renders it, to say the least, a doubtful compliment to him who has no right to the title.

Think like the wise; but talk like ordinary people. Never go out of the common road, but for somewhat.

Don't dispute against facts well established, merely because there is somewhat unaccountable in them. That the world should be created of nothing is to us inconceivable; but not therefore to be doubted.

As you are going to a party of mirth, think of the hazard you run of misbehaving. While you are engaged, do not wholly forget yourself. And after all is over, reflect how you have behaved. If well, be thankful; it is more than you could have promised. If otherwise, be more careful for the future.

It will never do to be ignorant of the names and approximate ages of great composers, especially in large cities, where music is so highly appreciated and so common a theme. It will be decidedly condemnatory if you talk of the *new* opera "Don Giovanni," or Rossini's "Trovatore," or are ignorant who composed "Fidelio," and in what opera occur such common pieces as "*Ciascun lo dice*," or "*Il Segreto*." I do not say that these trifles are indispensable, and when a man has better knowledge to offer, especially with genius or "cleverness" to back it, he will not only be pardoned for an ignorance of them, but can even take a high tone, and profess indifference or contempt of them. But, at the same time, such ignorance stamps an ordinary man, and hinders conversation.

Don't talk of "the opera" in the presence of those who are not frequenters of it. They will imagine that you are showing off, or that you are *lying*, and that you have never been to the opera twice in your life. For the same reason, avoid too frequently speaking of your acquaintance with celebrated men, unless you are a public man yourself, who would be supposed to have such acquaintance.

Do not sit dumb in company. That looks either like pride, cunning, or stupidity. Give your opinion modestly, but freely; hear that of others with candor; and ever endeavor to find out, and to communicate truth.

In mixed company, be readier to hear than to speak, and put people upon talking of what is in their own way. For then you will both oblige them, and be most likely to improve by their conversation.

Humanity will direct to be particularly cautious of treating with the least appearance of neglect those who have lately met with misfortunes, and are sunk in life. Such persons are apt to think themselves slighted, when no such thing is intended. Their minds being already sore, feel the least rub very severely. And who would be so cruel as to add affliction to the afflicted?

To smother the generosity of those who have obliged you, is imprudent, as well as ungrateful. The mention of kindnesses received may excite those who hear it to deserve your good word, by imitating the example which they see does others so much honor.

Learning is like bank-notes. Prudence and good behavior are like silver, useful upon all occasions.

If you have been once in company with an idle person, it is enough. You need never go again. You have heard all he knows. And he has had no opportunity of learning anything new. For idle people make no improvments.

Deep learning will make you acceptable to the learned; but it is only an easy and obliging behavior, and entertaining conversation, that will make you agreeable in all companies.

Men repent speaking ten times for once that they repent keeping silence.

It is an advantage to have concealed one's opinion. For by that means you may change your judgment of things (which every wise man finds reason to do) and not be accused of fickleness.

There is hardly any bodily blemish, which a winning behavior will not conceal, or make tolerable; and there is no external grace, which ill-nature or affectation will not deform.

If you mean to make your side of the argument appear plausible, do not prejudice people against what you think truth by your passionate manner of defending it.

There is an affected humility more insufferable than downright pride, as hypocrisy is more abominable than libertinism. Take care that your virtues be genuine and unsophisticated.

Never ask anyone who is conversing with you to repeat his words. Nothing is ruder than to say, "Pardon me, will you repeat that sentence? I did not hear you at first," and thus imply that your attention was wandering when he first spoke.

When we speak of ourselves and another person, whether he is absent or present, propriety requires us to mention ourselves last. Thus we should say, *he and I, you and I.*

If a man is telling that which is as old as the hills, or which you believe to be false, the better way is to let him go on. Why should you refuse a man the pleasure of believing that he is telling you something which you never heard before? Besides, by refusing to believe him, or by telling him that his story is old, you not only mortify him, but the whole company is made uneasy, and, by sympathy, share his mortification.

Never notice it if others make mistakes in language. To notice by word or look such errors in those around you, is excessively ill-bred.

Avoid raillery and sarcasm in social parties. They are weapons which few can use; and because you happen to have a razor in your possession, that is no reason why you should be allowed to cut the throats of the rest who are unarmed. Malicious jests at the expense of those who are present or absent, show that he who uses them is devoid both of the instincts and habits of a *gentleman.* Where two individuals or the whole company agree to banter each other with good-natured sallies of wit, it is very pleasant, but the least taint of ill-nature spoils all.

If upon the entrance of a visitor you continue a conversation begun before, you should always explain the subject to the newcomer.

If there is anyone in the company whom you do not know, be careful how you let off any epigrams or pleasant little sarcasms. You might be very witty upon halters to a man whose father had been hanged. The first requisite for successful conversation is to know your company well.

Carefully avoid subjects which may be construed into personalities, and keep a strict reserve upon family matters. Avoid, if you can, seeing the skeleton in your friend's closet, but if it is paraded for your special benefit, regard it as a sacred confidence, and never betray your knowledge to a third party.

Listen attentively and patiently to what is said. It is a great and difficult talent to be a good listener, but it is one which the well-bred man has to acquire, at whatever pains. Do not anticipate the point of a story which another person is reciting, or take it from his lips to finish it in your own language. To do this is a great breach of etiquette.

Dr. Johnson, whose reputation as a *talker* was hardly less than that which he acquired as a writer, prided himself on the appositeness of his quotations, the choice of his words, and the correctness of his expressions. Had he lived in this "age of progress," he would have discovered that his lexicon was not only incomplete, but required numerous emendations. We can fancy the irritable moralist endeavoring to comprehend the idea which a young lady wishes to convey when she expresses the opinion that a bonnet is "*awful*," or that of a young gentleman, when he asserts that his coat is "*played out!*"

Avoid the use of proverbs in conversation, and all sorts of cant phrases. This error is, I believe, censured by Lord Chesterfield, and is one of the most offensively vulgar which a person can commit.

It is bad manners to satirize lawyers in the presence of lawyers, or doctors in the presence of one of that calling, and so of all the professions. Nor should you rail against bribery and corruption in the presence of politicians, (especially of a New York politician) or members of Congress, as they will have good reason to suppose that you are hinting at them. It is the aim of politeness to leave the arena of social intercourse untainted with any severity of language, or bitterness of feeling. There are places and occasions where wrong must be exposed and reproved, but it is an unpardonable piece of rudeness to attempt such things at your own or another's social party, where everything is carefully to be avoided that can in the least disturb the happiness of anyone. For this reason all kinds of controversies are, as a general rule, to be avoided at such times.

Any conversation (that is not interdicted by decency and propriety) which can be pleasing to the whole company, is desirable. Amusement, more than instruction even, is to be sought for in social parties. People are not supposed to come together on such occasions because they are ignorant and need teaching, but to seek amusement and relaxation from professional and daily cares. All the English books on etiquette tell you that "punning is scrupulously to be avoided as a species of ale-house wit," and a savage remark of Dr. Johnson is usually quoted on the subject. But punning is no more to be avoided than any other kind of wit; and if all wit is to be banished from the social circle, it will be left a stupid affair indeed. All kinds of wit, puns by no means excepted, give a delightful relish to social parties when they spring up naturally and spontaneously out of the themes of conversation. But for a man to be constantly straining himself to make jokes is to make himself ridiculous, and to annoy the whole company, and is, therefore, what no gentleman will be guilty of.

Talk as little of yourself as possible, or of any science or business in which you have acquired fame. There is a banker in New York who is always certain to occupy the time of every party he gets into, by talking of his *per cents*, and boasting that he *began life without a cent*—which every one readily believes; and if he were to add that he *began life in a pig-pen*, they would believe that too.

If you put on a proud carriage, people will want to know what there is in you to be proud of. And it is ten to one whether they value your accomplishments at the same rate as you. And the higher you aspire, they will be the more desirous to mortify you.

Nothing is more nauseous than apparent self-sufficiency. For it shows the company two things, which are extremely disagreeable: that you have a high opinion of yourself, and that you have comparatively a mean opinion of them.

It is the concussion of passions that produces a storm. Let an angry man alone, and he will cool off himself.

It is but seldom that very remarkable occurrences fall out in life. The evenness of your temper will be in most danger of being troubled by trifles which take you by surprise.

It is as obliging in company, especially of superiors, to listen attentively, as to talk entertainingly.

Don't think of knocking out another person's brains, because he differs in opinion from you. It will be as rational to knock yourself on the head, because you differ from yourself ten years ago.

If you want to gain any man's good opinion, take particular care how you behave, the first time you are in company with him. The light you appear in at first, to one who is neither inclined to think well or ill of you, will strongly prejudice him either for or against you.

Good humor is the only shield to keep off the darts of the satirical railer. If you have a quiver well stored, and are sure of hitting him between the joints of the harness, do not spare him. But you had better not bend your bow than miss your aim.

The modest man is seldom the object of envy.

In the company of ladies, do not labor to establish learned points by long-winded arguments. They do not care to take too much pains to find out truth.

You will forbear to interrupt a person who is telling a story, even though he is making historical mistakes in dates and facts. If he makes mistakes it is his own fault, and it is not your business to mortify him by attempting to correct his blunders in presence of those with whom he is ambitious to stand well.

In a dispute, if you cannot reconcile the parties, withdraw from them. You will surely make one enemy, perhaps two, by taking either side in an argument when the speakers have lost their temper.

Do not *dispute* in a party of ladies and gentlemen. If a gentleman advances an opinion which is different from ideas you are known to entertain, either appear not to have heard it, or differ with him as gently as possible. You will not say, "Sir, you are mistaken!" "Sir, you are wrong!" or that you "happen to know better," but you will rather use some such phrase as, "Pardon me—if I am not mistaken," etc. This will give him a chance to say some such civil thing as that he regrets to disagree with you; and if he has not the good manners to do it, you have, at any rate, established your own manners as those of a gentleman in the eyes of the company. And when you have done that, you need not trouble yourself about any opinions he may advance contrary to your own.

If you talk sentences, do not at the same time give yourself a magisterial air in doing it. An easy conversation is the only agreeable one, especially in mixed company.

Be sure of the fact, before you lose time in searching for a cause.

If you have a friend that will reprove your faults and foibles, consider you enjoy a blessing, which the king upon the throne cannot have.

In disputes upon moral or scientific points, ever let your aim be to come at truth, not to conquer your opponent. So you never shall be at a loss in losing the argument, and gaining a new discovery.

What may be very entertaining in company with ignorant people, may be tiresome to those who know more of the matter than yourself.

There is a sort of accidental and altogether equivocal type of city women, who never get into the country, but they employ their time in trying to astonish the country people with narrations of the fine things they left behind them in the city. If they have a dirty little closet, with ten valueless books in it, they will call it their *library*. If they have some small room, that is used as kitchen, parlor, and dining-room, they will magnify it into a *drawing-room*. And a hundred other *little* signs of their *grea* vulgarity they will constantly insist on exhibiting to their country auditors.

Put yourself on the same level as the person to whom you speak, and under penalty of being considered a pedantic idiot, refrain from explaining any expression or word that you may use.

If you are really a wit, remember that in conversation its true office consists more in finding it in others, than showing off a great deal of it yourself. He who goes out of your company pleased with himself is sure to be pleased with you. Even as great a man as Dr. Johnson once retired from a party where everybody had spent the evening in listening to him, and remarked, as he went out, "We have had a pleasant evening, and much excellent conversation."

If you happen to fall into company where the talk runs into party, obscenity, scandal, folly, or vice of any kind, you had better pass for morose or unsocial, among people whose good opinion is not worth having, than shock your own conscience by joining in conversation which you must disapprove of.

If you would have a right account of things from illiterate people, let them tell their story in their own way. If you put them upon talking according to logical rules, you will quite confound them.

I was much pleased with the saying of a gentleman, who was engaged in a friendly argument with another upon a point in morals. "You and I [says he to his antagonist] seem, as far as I hitherto understand, to differ considerably in our opinions. Let us, if you please, try wherein we can agree." The scheme in most disputes is to try who shall conquer, or confound the other. It is therefore no wonder that so little light is struck out in conversation, where a candid inquiry after truth is the least thing thought of.

By all means, shun the vulgar habit of joking at the expense of women. All such tricks as refusing a lady a piece of tongue, because "*women already have tongue enough,*" are as vulgar as they are old and stale. The man who does not respect woman, exposes himself to the suspicion of associating generally with the fallen portion of the sex. And besides, he has no right to make a respectable parlor or drawing-room the theater of such vulgar jokes and railing against the sex as go down in low society.

If a man complains to you of his wife, a woman of her husband, a parent of a child, or a child of a parent, be very cautious how you meddle between such near relations, to blame the behavior of one to the other. You will only have the hatred of both parties, and do no good with either. But this does not hinder your giving both parties, or either, your best advice in a prudent manner.

Be prudently secret. But don't affect to make a secret of what all the world may know, nor give yourself airs of being as close as a conspirator. You will better disappoint idle curiosity by seeming to have nothing to conceal.

Never blame a friend without joining some commendation to make reproof go down.

It is by giving free rein to folly, in conversation and action, that people expose themselves to contempt and ridicule. The modest man may deprive himself of some part of the applause of some sort of people in conversation, by not shining altogether so much as he might have done. Or he may deprive himself of some lesser advantages in life by his reluctancy in putting himself forward. But it is only the rash and impetuous talker, or actor, that effectually exposes himself in company, or ruins himself in life. It is therefore easy to determine which is the safest side to err on.

It is a base temper in mankind, that they will net take the smallest slight at the hand of those who have done them the greatest kindness.

If you fall into the greatest company, in a natural and unforced way, look upon yourself as one of them; and do not sneak, nor suffer anyone to treat you unworthily, without just showing that you know behavior. But if you see them disposed to be rude, overbearing, or purse-proud, it will be more decent and less troublesome to retire, than to wrangle with them.

There cannot be any practice more offensive than that of taking a person aside to whisper in a room with company; yet this rudeness is of frequent occurrence—and that, with those who know it to be improper.

If at any time you chance, in conversation, to get on a side of an argument which you find not to be tenable, or any other way over-shoot yourself, turn off the subject in as easy and good humored a way as you can. If you proceed still, and endeavor, right or wrong, to make your first point good, you will only entangle yourself the more, and in the end expose yourself.

Never over-praise any absent person, especially ladies, in company of ladies. It is the way to bring envy and hatred upon those whom you wish well to.

To try whether your conversation is likely to be acceptable to people of sense, imagine what you say written down, or printed, and consider how it would read; whether it would appear natural, improving and entertaining; or affected, unmeaning, or mischievous.

It is better, in conversation with positive men, to turn off the subject in dispute with some merry conceit, than keep up the contention to the disturbance of the company.

Don't give your advice upon any extraordinary emergency, nor your opinion upon any difficult point, especially in company of eminent persons, without first taking time to deliberate. If you say nothing, it may not be known whether your silence was owing to the ignorance of the subject, or to modesty. If you give a rash and crude opinion, you are effectually and irrecoverably exposed.

If you fill your fancy, while you are in company, with suspicions of their thinking meanly of you; if you puff yourself up with imaginations of appearing to them a very witty, or profound person; if you discompose yourself with fears of misbehaving before them, or in any way put yourself out of yourself, you will not appear in your natural color, but in that of an affected, personated character, which is always disagreeable.

It may be useful to study, at leisure, a variety of proper phrases for such occasions as are most frequent in life, as civilities to superiors, expressions of kindness to inferiors; congratulations, condolence, expressions of gratitude, acknowledgment of faults, asking or denying of favors, etc. I prescribe no particular phrases, because, our language continually fluctuating, they must soon become stiff and unfashionable. The best method of acquiring the accomplishment of graceful and easy manner of expression for the common occasions of life, is attention and imitation of well-bred people. Nothing makes a man appear more contemptible than barrenness, pedantry, or impropriety of expression.

Avoid flattery. A delicate compliment is permissible in conversation, but flattery is broad, coarse, and to sensible people, disgusting. If you flatter your superiors, they will distrust you, thinking you have some selfish end; if you flatter ladies, they will despise you, thinking you have no other conversation.

If you meet an ill-bred fellow in company, whose voice and manners are offensive to you, you cannot resent it at the time, because by so doing you compel the whole company to be spectators of your quarrel, and the pleasure of the party would be spoiled.

If you must speak upon a difficult point, be the last speaker if you can.

You will not be agreeable to company, if you strive to bring in or keep up a subject unsuitable to their capacities, or humor.

You will never convince a man of ordinary sense by over-bearing his understanding. If you dispute with him in such a manner as to show a due deference for his judgment, your complaisance may win him, though your saucy arguments could not.

Avoid appearing dogmatical and too positive in any assertions you make, which can possibly be subject to any contradiction. He that is peremptory in his own story, may meet with another as positive as himself to contradict him, and then the two Sir Positives will be sure to have a skirmish.

The frequent use of the name of God, or the Devil; allusions to passages of Scripture; mocking at anything serious and devout, oaths, vulgar by-words, cant phrases, affected hard words, when familiar terms will do as well; scraps of *Latin*, *Greek* or *French;* quotations from plays spoke in a theatrical manner—all these, much used in conversation, render a person very contemptible to grave and wise men.

If you send people away from your company well-pleased with themselves, you need not fear but they will be well enough pleased with you, whether they have received any instruction from you or not. Most people had rather be pleased than instructed.

If you can express yourself to be perfectly understood in ten words, never use a dozen. Go not about to prove, by a long series of reasoning, what all the world is ready to own.

If anyone takes the trouble of finding fault with you, you ought in reason to suppose he has some regard for you, else he would not run the hazard of disobliging you, and drawing upon himself your hatred.

Do not ruffle or provoke any man; why should anyone be the worse for coming into company with you? Be not yourself provoked. Why should you give any man the advantage over you?

To say that one has opinions very different from those commonly received, is saying that he either loves singularity, or that he thinks for himself. Which of the two is the case, can only be found by examining the grounds of his opinions.

Don't appear to the public too sure, or too eager upon any project. If it should miscarry, which it is a chance but it does, you will be laughed at. The surest way to prevent which, is not to tell your designs or prospects in life.

If you give yourself a loose tongue in company, you may almost depend on being pulled to pieces as soon as your back *is* turned, however they may seem entertained with your conversation.

For common conversation, men of ordinary abilities will upon occasion do well enough. And you may always pick something out of any man's discourse, by which you may profit. For an intimate friend to improve by, you must search half a country over, and be glad if you can find him at last.

Don't give your time to every superficial acquaintance: it is bestowing what is to you of inestimable worth, upon one who is not likely to be the better for it.

If a person has behaved to you in an unaccountable manner, don't at once conclude him a bad man, unless you find his character given up by all who know him, nor then, unless the facts alleged against him be undoubtedly proved, and wholly inexcusable. But this is not advising you to trust a person whose character you have any reason to suspect. Nothing can be more absurd than the common way of fixing people's characters. Such a one has disobliged me, therefore he is a villain. Such another has done me a kindness, therefore he is a saint.

Superficial people are more agreeable the first time you are in their company, than ever afterwards. Men of judgment improve every succeeding conversation; beware therefore of judging by one interview.

You will not anger a man so much by showing him that you hate him, as by expressing a contempt of him.

Most women had rather have any of their good qualities slighted, than their beauty. Yet that is the most inconsiderable accomplishment of a woman of real merit.

You will be always reckoned by the world nearly of the same character with those whose company you keep.

You will please so much the less, if you go into company determined to shine. Let your conversation appear to rise out of thoughts suggested by the occasion, not strained or premeditated: nature always pleases; affectation is always odious.

ON DRESS

It is hardly necessary to remind the reader that dress, though often considered a trifling matter, is one of considerable importance, for a man's personal appearance is a sort of "index and obscure prologue" to his character.

Lord Chesterfield has said, "I cannot help forming some opinion of a man's sense and character from his dress." Besides, the appearance of a well-dressed man commands a certain degree of respect which would never be shown to a sloven. As Shakespeare has written, "The world is still deceived by ornament;" and there are those who associate fine clothes with fine people so strongly, that they do not trouble themselves to ascertain whether the wearers are worthy of respect, as others form their opinions of books by the gilding of the leaves and beauty of the binding.

The dress of a gentleman should be such as not to excite any special observation, unless it be for neatness and propriety. The utmost care should be exercised to avoid even the appearance of desiring to attract attention by the peculiar formation of any article of attire, or by the display of an immoderate quantity of jewelry, both being a positive evidence of vulgarity. His dress should be studiously neat, leaving no other impression than that of a well-dressed gentleman.

Well-bred people do not often dress in what is called "the height of the fashion," as that is generally left to dandies and pretenders. But still it is undoubtedly a great point gained to be well dressed. To be fancifully dressed, in gaudy colors, is to be very badly dressed, however, and is an example of ill taste which is rarely met with among people of substantial good breeding.

Cleanliness and neatness are the invariable accompaniments of good breeding. Every gentleman may not be dressed expensively, he may not be able to do so; but water is cheap, and no gentleman will ever go into company un-mindul of cleanliness either in his person or apparel.

A well-dressed man does not require so much an extensive as a varied wardrobe. He wants a different costume for every season and every occasion; but if what he selects is simple rather than striking, he may appear in the same clothes as often as he likes, as long as they are fresh and appropriate to the season and the object. There are four kinds of coats which he must have: a business coat, a frock-coat, a dress-coat, and an over-coat. A well dressed man may do well with four of the first, and one of each of the others per annum. An economical man can get along with less.

Did any lady ever see a gentleman with an embroidered waistcoat, and a profusion of chains, rings, and trinkets adorning his person?

Avoid affecting singularity in dress. Expensive dressing is no sign of a gentleman. If a gentleman is able to dress expensively it is very well for him to do so, but if *he is not able* to wear ten-dollar broadcloth, he may comfort himself with the reflection that cloth which costs but five dollars a yard will look quite as well when made into a well-fitting coat. With this suit, and well-made shoes, clean gloves, a white pocket-handkerchief, and an easy and graceful deportment withal, he may pass muster as a gentleman. Manners do quite as much to set off a suit of clothes as clothes do to set off a graceful person.

A dress perfectly suited to a tall, good-looking man, may render one who is neither ridiculous; as although the former may wear a remarkable waistcoat or singular coat, *almost* with impunity, the latter, by adopting a similiar costume, exposes himself to the laughter of all who see him. An unassuming simplicity in dress should always be preferred, as it prepossesses every one in favor of the wearer.

Avoid what is called the "ruffianly style of dress," or the *nonchalant* and *slouching* appearance of a half-unbuttoned vest, and suspenderless pantaloons. That sort of affectation is if possible even more disgusting than the painfully elaborate frippery of the dandy.

Gentlemen never make any display of jewelry; that is given up entirely to the dominion of female taste. But ladies of good taste seldom wear it in the morning. It is reserved for evening display and for brilliant parties.

The native independence of American character regards with disdain many of the stringent social laws which are recognized in England and on the continent. Thus, the dress which many of our countrymen adopt for the assembly-room and private parties would subject them to serious annoyance abroad. A frock-coat would not be tolerated a moment in any fashionable society in Europe, and whether it be esteemed a prejudice or otherwise, we are free to confess that in our opinion it is a violation of good taste, and unsuited either to a ball-room or private assembly.

We should, however, be far from denying the claim of gentleman to any person, simply because he wore a frock-coat; for the fickle goddess, Fashion, tolerates it to a certain extent in America; but if the universal custom among the refined and polished members of society were to exclude it, as in Europe, its use would manifest a contempt for the opinion of others, of which no gentleman could be guilty.

If the title of gentleman should depend entirely and solely on one's conformation to the laws of etiquette, the most unprincipled profligate or debauchee might successfully wear it; it is, however, but the finish and polish of the jewel—not the diamond itself.

If we were allowed to say anything to the ladies concerning dress in a dictatorial way, and were sure of being obeyed, we should order them generally to dress *less*. How often do we see a female attired in the height of fashion, perfectly gorgeous in costume, sweeping along the dusty street, perspiring under the weight of her finery—dressed, in fact, in a manner fit only for a carriage. This is a very mistaken and absurd fashion, and such people would be astonished to see the simplicity of real aristocracy as regards dress.

In our allusions to the dress of a gentleman, we have urged a studied simplicity of apparel; the same remarks are equally applicable to that of a lady. Indeed, *simplicity* is the grand secret of a lady's toilet. When she burdens herself with a profusion of *bijouterie* she rather detracts from than adds to her personal appearance, while all *outré* fashions and ultra styles of dress, though they excite attention, neither win respect nor enhance the attraction of the wearer.

Some ladies, perhaps imagining that they are deficient in personal charms—and we are willing to believe that there are such, although the Chesterfieldian school of philosophers would ridicule the idea—endeavor to make their clothes the spell of their attraction. With this end in view, they labor by lavish expenditure to supply in expensive adornment what they lack in beauty of form or feature. Unfortunately for their success, elegant dressing does not depend upon expense. A lady might wear the costliest silks that Italy could produce, adorn herself with laces from Brussels which years of patient toil are required to fabricate; she might carry the jewels of an Eastern princess around her neck and upon her wrists and fingers, yet still, in appearance, be essentially vulgar.

These were as nothing without grace, without adaptation, without a harmonious blending of colors, without the exercise of discrimination and good taste.

The most appropriate and becoming dress is that which so harmonizes with the figure as to make the apparel unobserved. When any particular portion of it excites the attention, there is a defect, for the details should not present themselves first but the result of perfect dressing should be an *elegant woman*, the dress commanding no especial regard. Men are but indifferent judges of the material of a lady's dress; in fact, they care nothing about the matter. A modest countenance and pleasing figure, habited in an inexpensive attire, would win more attention from men, than awkwardness and effrontery, clad in the richest satins of Stewart and the costliest gems of Tiffany.

There are occasionally to be found among both sexes, persons who neglect their dress through a ridiculous affectation of singularity, and who take pride in being thought utterly indifferent to their personal appearance. Millionaires are very apt to manifest this characteristic, but with them it generally arises through a miserly penuriousness of disposition; their imitators, however, are even more deficient than they in common sense.

Lavater has urged that persons habitually attentive to their attire, display the same regularity in their domestic affairs. He also says: "Young women who neglect their toilet and manifest little concern about dress, indicate a general disregard of order—a mind but ill adapted to the details of housekeeping—a deficiency of taste and of the qualities that inspire love."

Hence the desire of exhibiting an amiable exterior is essentially requisite in a young lady, for it indicates cleanliness, sweetness, a love of order and propriety, and all those virtues which are attractive to their associates, and particularly to those of the other sex.

Chesterfield asserts that a sympathy goes through every action of our lives, and that he could not help conceiving some idea of people's sense and character from the dress in which they appeared when introduced to him.

Another writer has remarked that he never yet met with a woman whose general style of dress was chaste, elegant, and appropriate, that he did not find her on further acquaintance to be, in disposition and mind, an object to admire and love.

The fair sex have the reputation of being passionately fond of dress, and the love of it has been said to be natural to women. We are not disposed to deny it, but we do not regard it as a weakness nor a peculiarity to be condemned. Dress is the appropriate finish of beauty. Someone has said that, "Without dress a handsome person is a gem, but a gem that is not set. But dress," he further remarks, "must be consistent with the graces and with nature."

"Taste," says a celebrated divine, "requires a congruity between the internal character and the external appearance; the imagination will involuntarily form to itself an idea of such a correspondence. First ideas are, in general, of considerable consequence. I should therefore think it wise in the female world to take care that their *appearance* should not convey a forbidding idea to the most superficial observer."

As we have already remarked, the secret of perfect dressing is simplicity, costliness being no essential element of real elegance. We have to add that everything depends upon the judgment and good taste of the wearer. These should always be a harmonious adaptation of one article of attire to another, as also to the size, figure, and complexion of the wearer. There should be a correspondence in all parts of a lady's toilet, so as to present a perfect entirety. Thus, when we see a female of light, delicate complexion, penciling her eyebrows until they are positively black, we cannot but entertain a contempt for her lack of taste and good sense. There is a harmony in nature's tints which art can never equal, much less improve.

A fair face is generally accompanied by blue eyes, light hair, eyebrows, and lashes. There is a delicacy and harmonious blending of correspondences which are in perfect keeping; but if you sully the eyebrows with blackness, you destroy all similitude of feature and expression, and almost present a deformity.

We cannot but allude to the practice of using white paints, a habit strongly to be condemned. If for no other reason than that poison lurks beneath every layer, inducing paralytic affections and premature death, they should be discarded—but they are a disguise which deceives no one, even at a distance; there is a ghastly deathliness in the appearance of the skin after it has been painted, which is far removed from the natural hue of health.

The hostess should be particularly careful not to outshine her guests. We have seen many instances where a lady, fond of dress, (and what lady is not fond of dress?)

and conscious that it is unbecoming to dress to excess when visitors are invited, yet so unable to restrain the desire of display, has made the whole of her guests look shabby, by the contrast of her own gay colors. To dress meanly is a mark of disrespect to the company, but it is equally so to make a very gay appearance. If you make a grand display yourself, you are apt to appear as if you wished to parade your appearance, and it is always safer to be under than over the mark.

In going out, consider the sort of company you are likely to meet, and endeavor to assimilate to them as much as possible—for to make a great display elsewhere is an evidence of bad taste. But here if you miss the happy medium, dress above the mark rather than below it, for you may dress more out of doors than you may at home. Where dancing is expected to take place, no one should go without new kid gloves; nothing is so revolting as to see one person in an assembly ungloved, especially where the heat of the room, and the exercise together, are sure to make the hands redder than usual. Always wear your gloves in church or in a theater.

We may add a few general maxims, applied to both sexes, and our task will be done.

"All affectation in dress," says Chesterfield, "implies a flaw in the understanding." One should, there-fore, avoid being singular, or attracting the notice, and the tongues of the sarcastic, by being eccentric.

Never dress against anyone. Choose those garments which suit you, and look well upon you, perfectly irrespective of the fact that a lady or gentleman in the same village or street may excel you.

When dressed for company, strive to appear as easy and natural as if you were in undress. Nothing is more distressing to a sensitive person, or more ridiculous to one gifted with an *esprit moqueur*, than to see a lady laboring under the consciousness of a fine gown; or a gentleman who is stiff, awkward, and ungainly in a brand-new coat.

Dress according to your age. It is both painful and ridiculous to see an old lady dressed as a belle of four-and-twenty, or an old fellow, old enough for a grandfather, affecting the costume and the manners of a *beau*.

Young men should be *well* dressed. Not foppishly, but neatly and well. An untidy person at five-and-twenty, degenerates, very frequently, into a sloven and a boor at fifty.

Be not too negligent, nor too studied in your attire; and lastly, let your behavior and conversation suit the clothes you wear, so that those who know you may feel that, after all, dress and external appearance is the least portion of a LADY or GENTLEMAN.

INTRODUCTIONS

THE custom which prevails in country places of introducing everybody you meet to each other, is both an annoying and an improper one. As a general rule, introductions ought not to be made, except where there is undoubted evidence that the acquaintance would be mutually agreeable and proper.

But if you should find an agreeable person in private society, who seems desirous of making your acquaintance, there cannot be any objection to your meeting his advances half way, although the ceremony of an "introduction" may not have taken place; his presence in your friend's house being a sufficient guarantee for his respectability, as of course if he were an improper person he would not be there.

It is customary in introducing people, to present the youngest person to the oldest, or the humblest to the highest in position, if there is any distinction.

In introducing a gentleman to a lady, address her first, thus: "Miss Mason, permit me to present you to Mr. Kent;" "Mr. Trevor, I have the pleasure of presenting to you Mr. Marlow." When one lady is married, and the other single, present the single lady to the matron—"Miss Harris, allow me to introduce you to Mrs. Martin."

When you introduce parties whom you are quite sure will be pleased with each other, it is well to add, after the introduction, that you take great pleasure in making them acquainted, which will be an assurance to each that you think they are well matched, and thus they are prepared to be friends from the start.

In introducing parties, be careful to pronounce each name distinctly, as there is nothing more awkward than to have one's name miscalled.

In introducing a foreigner, it is proper to present him as "Mr. Leslie, from England;" "Mr. La Hue from France." Likewise when presenting an American who has recently returned after traveling in distant lands, make him known as "Mr. Dunlap, lately from France," or "Mr. Meadows, recently from Italy."

It is very easy to make these slight specifications, and they at once afford an opening for conversation between the two strangers, for nothing will be more natural than to ask "the recently arrived" something about his voyage, or the places he has seen during his travels.

When presenting a governor, designate the State he governs—as, "Governor Fenton of New York." In introducing a member of Congress, mention the State to which he belongs, as "Mr. Sherman of Ohio," or "Mr. Banks of Massachusetts." Do not forget that Congress includes the two legislative bodies.

When introducing any of the members of your own family, mention the name in an audible tone. It is not considered sufficient to say "My father," "My mother," "My sister," or "My brother." But say, "My father, Mr. Stanley," "My brother, Mr. Weston," "My sister, Miss or Mrs. Hope." It is best to be explicit in all these things, for there may be more than one surname in the family. The eldest daughter should be introduced by her surname only, as, "Miss Sherwood," her younger sisters, as "Miss Maud Sherwood," "Miss Mary Sherwood."

In presenting a clergyman, do not neglect to put "Reverend" before his name. If he is a D. D. say, "The Reverend Doctor." If he is a bishop, then the word bishop is sufficient.

When you are introduced to a person, be careful not to appear as though you had never heard of him before. If he happens to be a person of any distinction, such a mistake would be unpardonable, and no person is complimented by being reminded of the fact that his name is unknown.

If by any misfortune you have been introduced to a person whose acquaintance you do not desire, you can merely make the formal bow of etiquette when you meet him, which, of itself, encourages no familiarity; but *the bow is indispensable*, for he cannot be thought a gentleman who would pass another with a vacant stare, after having been formally presented to him. By so doing, he would offer a slight which would justly make him appear contemptible even in the eyes of the person he means to humble.

What is called "cutting" another is never practiced by gentlemen or ladies, except in some extraordinary instances of bad conduct on the part of the individual thus sacrificed. An increased degree of ceremony and formal politeness is the most delicate way of withdrawing from an unpleasant acquaintance. Indeed, what is called "cutting" is rarely ever practiced by well-bred ladies and gentlemen.

On introduction in a room, a married lady generally offers her hand, a young lady not; in a ball-room, where the introduction is to dancing, not to friendship, you never shake hands; and as a general rule, an introduction is not followed by shaking hands—only by a bow. It may perhaps be laid down, that the more public the place of introduction, the less hand-shaking takes place; but if the introduction be particular, if it be accompanied by personal recommendation, such as, "I want you to know my friend Jones," then you give Jones your hand, and warmly too.

It is understood in society, that a person who has been *properly* introduced to you, has some claim on your good offices in future; you cannot therefore slight him without good reason, and the chance of being called to an account for it.

LETTERS OF INTRODUCTION

LETTERS of introduction are to be regarded as certificates of repectability, and are therefore never to be given where you do not feel sure on this point. To send a person of whom you know nothing into the confidence and family of a friend, is an unpardonable recklessness. In England, letters of introduction are called "tickets to soup," because it is generally customary to invite a gentleman to dine who comes with a letter of introduction to you. Such is also the practice, to some extent, in this country, but etiquette *here* does not make the dinner so essential as *there*.

In England, the party holding a letter of introduction never takes it himself to the party to whom it is addressed, but he sends it with his card of address.

In France, and on the continent of Europe generally, directly the reverse is the fashion. In America the English custom generally prevails; though where a young gentleman has a letter to one who is many years his senior, or to one whose aid he seeks in some enterprise, he takes it at once himself.

When a gentleman, bearing a letter of introduction to you, leaves his card, you should call on him, or send a note, as early as possible. There is no greater insult than to treat a letter of introduction with indifference—it is a slight to the stranger as well as to the introducer, which no subsequent attentions will cancel. After you have made this call, it is, to some extent, optional with you as to what further attentions you shall pay the party. In this country everybody is supposed to be very busy, which is always a sufficient excuse for not paying elaborate attentions to visitors. It is not demanded that any man shall neglect his business to wait upon visitors or guests.

Do not imagine these little ceremonies to be insignificant and beneath your attention; they are the customs of society; and if you do not conform to them, you will gain the unenviable distinction of being pointed out as an ignorant, ill-bred person. Not that you may *care* the more for strangers by showing them civility, but you should scrupulously avoid the imputation of being deficient in good-breeding; and if you do not choose to be polite for *their* sakes, you ought to be so for *your own*.

Letters of introduction should only be given by actual friends of the persons addressed, and to actual friends of their own. Never, if you are wise, give a letter to a person whom you do not know, nor address one to one whom you know slightly. The letter of introduction, if actually given to its bearer, should be left unsealed, that he may not incur the fate of the Persian messenger, who brought tablets of introduction recommending the new acquaintance to cut his head off. A letter of this kind must therefore be carefully worded, stating in full the name of the person introduced, but with as few remarks about him as possible. It is generally sufficient to say that he is a friend of yours, whom you trust your other friend will receive with attention, etc. In traveling it is well to have as many letters as possible, but not to pin your faith on them.

DINNER PARTIES

INVITATIONS to dine, from a married party, are sent in some such form as the following:

Mr. and Mrs. A——present their compliments to Mr. and Mrs. P——and request the honor, [or hope to have the pleasure] of their company to dinner on Wednesday, the 10th of December next, at seven.

A——Street, November 18th, 18—.

R. S. V. P.

The letters in the corner imply "*Répondez, s'il vous plait;*" meaning, "an answer will oblige." The reply, accepting the invitation, is concluded in the following terms:

Mr. and Mrs. B—— present their compliments to Mr. and Mrs. A——, and will do themselves the honor, [or will have much pleasure in] accepting their kind invitation to dinner on the 10th of December next.

B——Square, November 21st, 18—.

The answer to invitations to dine, accepting or declining, should be sent immediately, and are always addressed to the lady. If, after you have accepted an invitation, anything occurs to render it impossible for you to go, the lady should be informed of it immediately. It is a great breach of etiquette not to answer an invitation as soon after it is received as possible, and it is an insult to disappoint when we have promised.

Cards or invitations for a dinner party, should be issued at least two weeks beforehand, and care should be taken by the hostess, in the selection of the invited guests, that they should be suited to each other. Much also of the pleasure of the dinner-party will depend on the arrangement of the guests at table, so as to form a due admixture of talkers and listeners, the grave and the gay.

Letters or cards of invitation should always name the hour of dinner; and well-bred people will arrive as nearly at the specified time as they can. Be sure and not be a minute behind the time, and you should not get there long before, unless the invitation requests you particularly to come early for a little chat before dinner.

It is always best for the lady of the house, where a dinner-party is to come off, to be dressed and ready to appear in the drawing-room as early as possible, so that if any of the guests should happen to come a little early, she may be prepared to receive them. It is awkward for both parties where visitors arrive before the lady of the house is ready for them. If it is necessary for her to keep an eye upon the dinner, it is still best that she should familiarly receive her guests, and beg to be excused, if it is necessary for her to vanish occasionally to the kitchen. A real lady is not ashamed to have it known that she goes into the kitchen: on the contrary, it is more likely that she will be a little proud of being thought capable of superintending the preparing feast.

It is not in good taste for the lady of the house, where a dinner-party is given, to dress very much. She leaves it for her lady-guests to make what display they please, and she offers no rivalry to their fine things. She contents herself with a tasty *négligé*, which often proves the most fascinating equipment after all, especially, if the cheeks become a little flushed with natural bloom, in consequence of the exercise and anxiety incident to the reception of the guests.

The half hour before dinner has always been considered as the great ordeal through which the lady of the house, in giving a dinner-party, will either pass with flying colors, or lose many of her laurels. The anxiety to receive her guests, her hope that all will be present in good time, her trust in the skill of her cook, and the attention of the other domestics all tend to make the few minutes a trying time. The lady however, must display no kind of agitation, but show her tact in suggesting light and cheerful subjects of conversation, which will be much aided by the introduction of any particular new book, curiosity of art, or article of *virtu*, which may pleasantly engage the attention of the company.

"Waiting for dinner," however, is a trying time, and there are few who have not felt:

> How sad it is to sit and pine,
> The long *half-hoar* before we dine!

Upon our watches oft; we look,
Then wonder at the clock and cook,
And strive to laugh in spite of Fate!
But laughter forced, soon quits the room,
And leaves it to its former gloom.
But lo! the dinner now appears,
The object of our hope and fears,
The end of all our pain!

In giving an entertainment of this kind, the lady should remember that it is her duty to make her guests feel happy, comfortable, and quite at their ease; and the guests should also consider that they have come to the house of their hostess to be happy.

When dinner is on the table, the lady and gentleman of the house will have an opportunity of showing their tact by seeing that the most distinguished guests, or the *oldest*, are shown into the dining-room first, and by making those companions at the table who are most likely to be agreeable to each other. The lady of the house may lead the way, or follow her guests into the dining-room, as she pleases. Among those who delight to follow the etiquette of the English nobility, the latter practice is followed. But the practice must not be considered a test of good breeding in America. If the lady leads, the husband will follow behind the guests, with the lady on his arm who is to sit at his side. The old custom is still followed to some extent in this country, of the lady taking the head of the table, with the two most favored guests seated, the one at her right and the other at her left hand; while the gentleman of the house takes the foot of the table, supported on each side by the two ladies most entitled to consideration. But this old rule is by no means slavishly followed in polite society in this country.

In order to be able to watch the course of the dinner, and to see that nothing is wanting to their guests, the lady and gentleman of the house usually seat themselves, in the centre of the table, opposite each other.

When all the guests are seated, the lady of the house serves in plates, from a pile at her left hand, the soup, which she sends round, beginning with her neighbors right and left, and continuing till all are helped. These first plates usually pass twice, for each guest endeavors to induce his neighbor to accept what was sent to him.

The gentleman then carves, or causes to be carved by some expert guest, the large pieces, in order afterwards to do the other honors himself. If you have no skill in carving meats, do not attempt it; nor should you ever discharge this duty except when your good offices are solicited by him; neither can we refuse anything sent us from his hand.

HABITS AT TABLE

As soon as dinner is announced, the host or hostess will give the signal for leaving the drawing-room, and in all probability you will be requested to escort one of the ladies to the table. If this should occur, offer the lady your left arm, and at the table remain standing until every lady is seated, then take the place assigned to you by the hostess. When you leave the parlor, pass out first, and the lady will follow you, still lightly holding your arm. At the door of the dining-room, the lady will drop your arm. You should then pass in, and wait at one side of the entrance till she passes you. Having arrived at the table, each gentleman respectfully salutes the lady whom he conducts, who in her turn, also bows and takes her seat.

Nothing indicates the good breeding of a gentleman so much as his manners at table. There are a thousand little points to be observed, which, although not absolutely necessary, distinctly stamp the refined and well-bred man. A man may pass muster by *dressing well*, and may sustain himself tolerably in conversation; but if he be not perfectly "*au fait*," *dinner* will betray him.

Any unpleasant peculiarity, abruptness, or coarseness of manners, is especially offensive at table. People are more easily disgusted at that time than at any other. All such acts as leaning over on one side in your chair, placing your elbows on the table, or on the back of your neighbor's chair, gaping, twisting about restlessly in your seat, are to be avoided as heresies of the most infidel stamp at table.

Though the body at table should always be kept in a tolerably upright and easy position, yet one need not sit bolt-upright, as stiff and prim as a poker. To be easy, to be natural, and to appear comfortable, is the deportment required.

Always go to a dinner as neatly dressed as possible. The expensiveness of your apparel is not of much importance, but its freshness and cleanliness are indispensable. The hands and fingernails require especial attention. It is a great insult to every lady at the table for a man to sit down to dinner with his hands in a bad condition.

It is considered vulgar to take fish or soup twice. The *reason* for not being helped twice to fish or soup at a large dinner-party is, because by doing so you keep three parts of the company staring at you whilst waiting for the second course, which is spoiling, much to the annoyance of the mistress of the house. The selfish greediness, therefore, of so doing constitutes its vulgarity. At a family dinner it is of less importance, and is consequently often done.

You will sip your soup as quietly as possible from the side of the spoon, and you, of course, will not commit the vulgarity of blowing in it, or trying to cool it, after it is in your mouth, by drawing in an unusual quantity of air, for by so doing you would be sure to annoy, if you did not turn the stomach of the lady or gentleman next to you.

Be careful and do not touch either your knife or your fork until after you have finished eating your soup. Leave your spoon in your soup plate, that the servant may remove them.

Never *use your knife to convey* your food to your mouth, *under any circumstances;* it is unnecessary, and glaringly vulgar. Feed yourself with a *fork* or *spoon, nothing else*—a knife is only to be used for cutting.

If at dinner you are requested to help anyone to sauce, do not pour it over the meat or vegetables, but on one side. If you should have to carve and help a joint, do not load a person's plate—it is vulgar; also in serving soup, one ladleful to each plate is sufficient.

Fish should always be helped with a silver fish-slice, and your own portion of it divided by the fork aided by a piece of bread. The application of a knife to fish is likely to destroy the delicacy of its flavor; besides which, fish sauces are often acidulated; acids corrode steel, and draw from it a disagreeable taste.

The lady and gentleman of the house are, of course, helped last, and they are very particular to notice, every minute, whether the waiters are attentive to every guest. But they do not press people either to eat more than they appear to want, nor *insist* upon their partaking of any particular dish. It is allowable for you to recommend, so far as to say that it is considered "excellent," but remember that tastes differ, and dishes which suit *you*, may be unpleasant to others; and that, in consequence of your urgency, some modest people might feel themselves compelled to partake of what is disagreeable to them.

Neither ladies nor gentlemen ever wear gloves at table, unless their hands, from some cause, are not fit to be seen.

Avoid too slow or too rapid eating; the one will appear as though you did not like your dinner, and the other as though you were afraid you would not get enough.

Making a noise in chewing your food, or breathing hard in eating, are unseemly habits, which will be sure to get you a bad name at table, among people of good-breeding.

Let it be a sacred rule that *you cannot use your knife, or fork, or teeth too quietly.*

Avoid picking your teeth, if possible, at table, for however agreeable such a practice might be to yourself, it may be offensive to others. The habit which some have of holding one hand over the mouth, does not avoid the vulgarity of teeth-picking at table.

Unless you are requested to do so, never select any particular part of a dish; but if your host asks you what part you prefer, name some part, as in this case the incivility would consist in making your host choose as well as carve for you.

If your host or hostess passes you a plate, keep it, especially if you have chosen the food upon it, for others have also a choice, and by passing it, you may give your neighbor dishes distasteful to him, and take yourself those which he would much prefer.

If a dish is distasteful to you, decline it, but make no remarks about it. It is sickening and disgusting to explain at a table how one article makes you sick, or why some other dish has become distasteful to you. I have seen a well-dressed tempting dish go from a table untouched, because one of the company told a most digusting anecdote about finding vermin served in a similar dish.

If the meat or fish upon your plate is too rare or too well-done, do not eat it; give for an excuse that you prefer some other dish before you; but never tell your host that his cook has made the dish uneatable.

If a gentleman is seated by the side of a lady or elderly person, politeness requires him to save them all trouble of pouring out for themselves to drink, and of obtaining whatever they are in want of at the table. He should be eager to offer them whatever he thinks to be most to their taste.

Never pare an apple or a pear for a lady unless she desire you, and then be careful to use your fork to hold it; you may sometimes offer to *divide a very large pear* with or for a person.

It is not good taste to praise extravagantly every dish that is set before you; but if there are some things that are really very nice, it is well to speak in their praise. But, above all things, avoid seeming indifferent to the dinner that is provided for you, as that might be construed into a dissatisfaction with it.

Some persons, in helping their guests, or recommending dishes to their taste, preface every such action with a eulogy on its merits, and draw every bottle of wine with an account of its virtues; others, running into the contrary extreme, regret or fear that each dish is not exactly as it should be; that the cook, etc., etc. Both of these habits are grievous errors. You should leave it to your guests alone to approve, or suffer one of your intimate friends who is present, to vaunt your wine.

If you ask the waiter for anything, you will be careful to speak to him gently in the tone of *request*, and not of *command*. To speak to a waiter in a driving manner will create, among well-bred people, the suspicion that you were sometime a servant yourself, and are putting on *airs* at the thought of your promotion. Lord Chesterfield says: "If I tell a footman to bring me a glass of wine, in a rough, insulting manner, I should expect that, in obeying me, he would contrive to spill some of it upon me, and I am sure I should deserve it."

Should your servants break anything while you are at table, never turn round or inquire into the particulars, however annoyed you may feel. If your servants betray stupidity or awkwardness in waiting on your guests, avoid reprimanding them *publicly*, as it only draws attention to their errors, and adds to their embarrassment.

Never commit the vulgarism of speaking when you have any food in your mouth.

When you have occasion to change or pass your plate during dinner, be careful and remove your knife and fork, that the plate *alone* may be taken, but after you have finished your dinner, cross the knife and fork on the plate, that the servant may take all away, before bringing you clean ones for dessert.

Do not put butter on your bread at dinner, and avoid biting or cutting your bread from the slice, or roll; rather break off small pieces, and put these in your mouth with your fingers.

It is considered vulgar to dip a piece of bread into the preserves or gravy upon your plate and then bite it. If you desire to eat them together, it is much better to break the bread in small pieces, and convey these to your mouth with your fork.

Avoid putting bones, or the seeds of fruit, upon your table-cloth. Rather place them upon the edge of your plate.

When you wish to help yourself to butter, salt, or sugar, use the butter knife, salt spoon, and sugar tongs to use your own knife, spoon or fingers evinces great ignorance and ill-breeding.

It is customary in some American families to serve their guests with coffee in the parlor after dinner. But this is a European custom which is not generally practiced in polite American society. When coffee is given at the close of the dinner, it is more usual to serve it before the guests leave the table. The practice of handing it round in the parlor or drawing-room, is an unnecessary inconvenience to the guests particularly, without any compensating advantages.

Finger-glasses are generally handed round as soon as the viands are removed, but they are intended merely to wet the fingers and around the mouth. When the finger-glasses are passed, wet your fingers in them and then wipe them upon your napkin. The habit of rinsing the mouth at table is a disgusting piece of indelicacy, which is never practiced by any well-bred person.

Upon leaving the table, lay your napkin beside your plate, but do not fold it.

Do not leave the table until the lady of the house gives the signal, and when you leave offer your arm to the lady whom you escorted to the table.

It is generally the custom in this country for ladies to retain their seats at table till the end of the feast, but if they withdraw, the gentlemen all rise when they leave the table, and remain standing until they have left the room.

Politeness demands that you remain at least an hour in the parlor, after dinner; and, if you can dispose of an entire evening, it would be well to devote it to the person who has entertained you. It is excessively rude to leave the house as soon as dinner is over.

WINE AT TABLE

ALMOST every gentleman has wine at his table whenever he has invited guests. Indeed, wine is considered an indispensable part of a good dinner, to which ladies and gentlemen have been formally invited. Even if you are a total-abstinence man yourself, you will not, if you are really a gentleman, attempt to compel all your guests to be so against their wish. If you are so fanatical that you have what is called "conscientious scruples" against furnishing wine, then you should invite none to dine who are not as fanatical and bigoted as yourself. You must consider that a gentleman may have "conscientious scruples" against dining with you on cold water, for there are even temperate and sober gentleman who would go without meat as soon as be deprived of their glass of wine at dinner. The vegetarian, who would force his guests to dine on cabbages and onions, is hardly guilty of a greater breach of etiquette than the total-abstinence fanatic who would compel his guests to go without wine.

If there is a gentleman at the table who is known to be a total-abstinence man, you will not urge him to drink. He will suffer his glass to be filled at the first passage of the wine, and raising it to his lips, will bow his respects with the rest of the guests, and after that his glass will be allowed to remain untouched. As little notice as possible should be taken of his total-abstinence peculiarity. And, if he is a gentleman, he will carefully avoid drawing attention to it himself .

It is not now the custom to ask a lady across the table to take wine with you. It is expected that every lady will be properly helped to wine by the gentleman who takes her to the table, or who sits next to her. But if you are in company where the old custom prevails, it would be better breeding to follow the custom of the place, rather than by an omission of what your entertainer considers civility, to prove him, in face of his guests, to be either ignorant or vulgar. If either a lady or gentleman is invited to take wine at table, they must *never refuse;* if they do not *drink,* they need only touch the wine to their lips. Do not offer to help a lady to wine until you see she has finished her soup or fish.

Always wipe your mouth before drinking, as nothing is more ill-bred than to grease your glass with your lips.

Do not propose to take wine with your host; it is his privilege to invite you.

It is considered well bred to take the same wine as that selected by the person with whom you drink. When, however, the wine chosen by him is unpalatable to you, it is allowable to take that which you prefer, at the same time apologizingly saying, "Will you permit me to drink *claret?*" or whatever wine you have selected.

In inviting a lady to take wine with you at table, you should politely say, "Shall I have the pleasure of a glass of wine with you?" You will then either hand her the bottle you have selected, or send it by the waiter, and afterwards fill your own glass, when you will politely and silently bow to each other, as you raise the wine to your lips. The same ceremony is to be observed when inviting a gentleman.

On raising the first glass of wine to his lips, it is customary for a gentleman to bow to the lady of the house.

It is not customary to propose *toasts* or to drink deep at a gentleman's family table. Lord Byron describes "a largish party," as "first silent, then talky, then argumentative, then disputatious, then unintelligible, then altogethery, then drunk." But this was "a largish party," which, it is to be hoped, was given at a tavern; for the man who drinks to intoxication, or to any considerable degree of *elevation,* at a gentleman's family table, ought never to expect to be invited a second time.

At dinner parties which are given to gentlemen, for the purpose of conviviality, one may indulge in as much wine as he pleases, provided he does not get *drunk,* and make a nuisance of himself. Where drinking, and toasting, and bumpers, are the order of the feast, as at a public dinner, given in honor of a distinguished man, or at the inauguration of some public enterprise, far greater latitude is all lowed, in all things, than on more private and select occasions.

In conclusion of our article on table etiquette, we quote from a recent English work, some humorous, but valuable hints:

"We now come to habits at table, which are very important. However agreeable a man maybe in society, if he offends or disgusts by his table traits, he will soon be scouted from it, and justly so. There are some broad rules for behavior at table. Whenever there is a servant to help you, never help yourself. Never put a knife into your mouth, not even with cheese, which should be eaten with a fork. Never use a spoon for anything but liquids. Never touch anything edible with your fingers.

"Forks were undoubtedly a later invention than fingers, but as we are not cannibals, I am inclined to think they were a good one. There are some few things which you may take up with your fingers. Thus an epicure will eat even macaroni with his fingers; and as sucking asparagus is more pleasant than chewing it, you may, as an epicure, take it up *au naturel*. But both these things are generally eaten with a fork. Bread is, of course, eaten with the fingers, and it would be absurd to carve it with your knife and fork. It must, on the contrary, always be broken when not buttered, and you should never put a slice of dry bread to your mouth to bite a piece off. Most fresh fruit, too, is eaten with the natural prongs, but when you have peeled an orange or apple, you should cut it with the aid of the fork, unless you can succeed in breaking it. Apropos of which, I may hint that no epicure ever yet put a knife to an apple, and that an orange should be peeled with a spoon. But the art of peeling an orange so as to hold its own juice, and its own sugar too, is one that can scarcely be taught in a book.

"However, let us go to dinner, and I will soon tell you whether you are a well-bred man or not; and here let me premise that what is good manners for a small dinner is good manners for a large one, and *vice versa*. Now, the first thing you do is to sit down. Stop, sir! pray do not cram yourself into the table in that way; no, nor sit a yard from it, like that. How graceless, inconvenient, and in the way of conversation! Why, dear me! you are positively putting your elbows on the table, and now you have got your hands fumbling about with the spoons and forks, and now you are nearly knocking my new hock glasses over. Can't you take your hands down, sir? Didn't you, learn that in the nursery? Didn't your mamma say to you, 'Never put your hands above the table except to carve or eat?' Oh! but come, no nonsense, sit up, if you please. I can't have your fine head of hair forming a side dish on my table; you must not bury your face in the plate; you came to show it, and it ought to be alive. Well, but there is no occasion to throw your head back like that, you look like an alderman, sir, *after* dinner. Pray, don't lounge in that sleepy way. You are here to eat, drink, and be merry. You can sleep when you get home.

"Well, then, I suppose you can see your napkin. Got none, indeed! Very likely, in *my* house. You may be sure that I never sit down to a meal without napkins. I don't want to make my tablecloths unfit for use, and I don't want to make my trousers unwearable. Well, now, we are all seated, you can unfold it on your knees; no, no;

don't tuck it into your waistcoat like an alderman; and what! what on earth do you mean by wiping your forehead with it? Do you take it for a towel? Well, never mind, I am consoled that you did not go farther, and use it as a pocket-handkerchief. So talk away to the lady on your right, and wait till soup is handed to you. By the way, that waiting is the most important part of table manners, and, as much as possible, you should avoid asking for anything or helping yourself from the table. Your soup you eat with a spoon—I don't know what else you *could* eat it with—but then it must be one of good size. Yes, that will do, but I beg you will not make that odious noise in drinking your soup. It is louder than a dog lapping water, and a cat would be quite genteel to it. Then you need not scrape up the plate in that way, nor even tilt it to get the last drop. I shall be happy to send you some more; but I must just remark, that it is not the custom to take two helpings of soup, and it is liable to keep other people waiting, which, once for all, is a selfish and intolerable habit. But don't you hear the servant offering you sherry? I wish you would attend, for my servants have quite enough to do, and can't wait all the evening while you finish that very mild story to Miss Goggles. Come, leave that decanter alone. I had the wine put on the table to fill up; the servants will hand it directly, or, as we are a small party, I will tell you to help yourself; but pray, do not be so officious. (There, I have sent him some turbot to keep him quiet. I declare he cannot make up his mind.) You are keeping my servant again, sir. Will you, or will you not, do turbot? Don't examine it in that way; it is quite fresh, I assure you; take or decline it. Ah, you take it, but that is no reason why you should take up a knife too. Fish, I repeat, must never be touched with a knife. Take a fork in the right and a small piece of bread in the left hand. Good, but——? Oh! that is atrocious; of course you must not swallow the bones, but you should rather do so than spit them out in that way. Put up your napkin like this, and land the said bone on your plate. Don't rub your head in the sauce, my good man, nor go progging about after the shrimps or oysters therein. Oh! how horrid! I declare your mouth was wide open and full of fish. Small pieces, I beseech you; and once for all, whatever you eat, keep your mouth *shut*, and never attempt to talk with it full.

"So now you have got a pâté. Surely you are not taking two on your plate! There is plenty of dinner to come, and one is quite enough. Oh! dear me, you are incorrigible. What! a knife to cut that light brittle pastry? No, nor fingers, never. Nor a spoon—almost as bad. Take your fork, sir, your fork; and, now you have eaten, oblige me by wiping your mouth and moustache with your napkin, for there is a bit of the pastry hanging to the latter, and looking very disagreeable. Well, you can refuse a dish if you like. There is no positive necessity for you to take venison if you don't want it. But, at any rate, do not be in that terrific hurry. You are not going off by the next train. Wait for the sauce and wait for the vegetables; but whether you eat them or not, do not begin before everybody else. Surely you must take my table for that of a railway refreshment-room, for you have finished before the person I helped first. Fast eating is bad for the digestion, my good sir, and not very good manners either.

"What! are you trying to eat meat with a fork alone? Oh! it is sweetbread; I beg your pardon, you are quite right. Let me give you a rule: Everything that can be cut without a knife, should be cut with a fork alone. Eat your vegetables, therefore, with a fork. No, there is no necessity to take a spoon for peas; a fork in the right hand will do. What! did I really see you put your knife into your mouth? Then I must give you up. Once for all, and ever, the knife is to cut, not to help with. Pray, do not munch in that noisy manner; chew your food well, but softly. *Eat slowly.* Have you not heard that Napoleon lost the battle of Leipsie by eating too fast? It is a fact though. His haste caused indigestion, which made him incapable of attending to the details of the battle. You see you are the last person eating at table. Sir, I will not allow you to speak to my servants in that way. If they are so remiss as to oblige you to ask for anything, do it gently, and in a low tone, and thank a servant just as much as you would his master. Ten to one he is as good a man; and because he is your inferior in position, is the very reason you should treat him courteously. Oh! it is of no use to ask me to take wine; far from pacifying me, it will only make me more angry, for I tell you the custom is quite gone out, except in a few country villages, and at a mess-table. Nor need you ask the lady to do so. However, there is this consolation, if you should ask anyone to take wine with you, he or she *cannot* refuse, so you have your own way. Perhaps next you will be asking me to hob and nob, or *trinquer* in the French fashion with arms encircled. Ah! you don't know, perhaps, that when a lady *trinques* in that way with you, you have a right to finish off with a kiss. Very likely, indeed! But it *is* the custom in familiar circles in France, but then we are not Frenchmen. *Will* you attend to your lady, sir? You did not come merely to eat, but to make yourself agreeable. Don't sit as glum as the Memnon at Thebes; talk and be pleasant. Now you have some pudding. No knife—no, *no*. A spoon, if you like, but better still, a fork. Yes, ice requires a spoon; there is a small one handed you, take that.

"Say 'no.' This is the fourth time wine has been handed to you, and I am sure you have had enough. Decline this time if you please. Decline that dish too. Are you going to eat of everything that is handed? I pity you if you do. No, you must not ask for more cheese, and you must eat it with your fork. Break the rusk with your fingers. Good. You are drinking a glass of old port. Do not quaff it down at a gulp in that way. Never drink a whole glassful of anything at once.

"Well, here is the wine and dessert. Take whichever wine you like, but remember you must keep to that, and not change about. Before you go up stairs I will allow you a glass of sherry after your claret, but otherwise drink of one wine only! You don't mean to say you are helping yourself to wine before the ladies! At least, offer it to the one next to you, and then pass it on, gently, not with a push like that. Do not drink so fast; you will hurry me in passing the decanters, if I see that your glass is empty. You need not eat dessert till the ladies are gone, but offer them whatever is nearest to you. And now they are gone, draw your chair near mine, and I will try and talk more pleasantly to you. You will come out admirably at your next dinner with all my teaching. What! you are excited, you are talking loud to the colonel. Nonsense! Come and talk easily to me or to your nearest neighbor. There, don't drink any more wine, for I see you are getting romantic. You oblige me to make a move. You have had enough of those walnuts; you are keeping me, my dear sir. So now to coffee [one cup] and tea, which I beg you will not pour into your saucer to cool. Well, the dinner has done you good, and me too. Let us be amiable to the ladies, but not too much so."

CARVING

CARVING is an art winch every parent should teach his sons and daughters. Nothing can be more disagreeable and unpleasant than to be placed before any particular dish without being able to help it properly. It is generally the case when the head of the family is a good carver; for he so objects to see things badly cut, that he prefers carving everything himself. We remember once, when very young, being invited to a large dinner, and we were placed before a ham. We began to hack this article, when the general, the founder of the feast, said to his servant, "Take that ham away from that young gentleman, and place it before Someone who knows how to carve." From that moment we determined to achieve the art of carving, and after great difficulty we succeeded, and succeeded so well that once, in carving a hare, a clergyman, one of the guests, remarked what an excellent invention that of boning a hare was, we carved it with so much ease; but determined to have a joke at the expense of the clergyman, we laid down the knife and fork, and said, "Sir, we are surprised that you could express such an opinion, when it is well known that it has filled more jails and sent more men to the treadmill than any other thing you can name," "What, sir, taking the bones out of a hare?" "No, sir, 'boning' the hare first." No one can carve without practice, and consequently children ought to begin young, in order to acquire a thorough knowledge of the art. It is difficult to describe the method of carving, even with drawings or diagrams; but the reader who wishes to learn, may, by observing how good carvers proceed, and applying what he has seen to what he reads, with practice, soon become an adept.

And first, never stand up to carve; this is the greatest vulgarity, and even a very short man need not stand up. A little, deformed, hump-back friend of ours, used to give very good dinners; he carved well, and delighted in showing it, but he had a failing—always to have very large joints of meat before him. One day a stranger guest arrived late, dinner had been served, even soup and fish had been removed; the host was absolutely hidden behind an enormous round of beef, and the stranger saw nothing at the head of the table but the monstrous joint, round which a knife was revolving with wonderful rapidity. Steam was the subject of talk at the moment, and he exclaimed, "I did not know that you had brought steam to this perfection." "What perfection?" "Why, don't you see that round of beef is carved by steam." This was enough; it got the hunchback's steam up, and, jumping on the chair, he demanded who dare insult him in his own house; and it was with great difficulty that his friends could appease his wrath, and turn his steam off. Ever since the time of Adam, men and women have been prone to excuse themselves and lay the blame on others. Thus, a person who could not swim, complained bitterly of the want of buoyancy in the water; and another, who had frightfully mangled a leg of mutton in attempting to carve, declared that the sheep was deformed and had a bandy leg.

In France, at all large dinners, dishes are carved at the sideboard by a servant, and then handed round in small portions. It saves a great deal of trouble, and prevents the shower of gravy with which awkward carvers will often inundate the table cloth, and sometimes their neighbors. It would be well if this custom was universal in America, where it is rare to find good carver. In helping the soup, never say, "Will you let me assist you to some of this soup?" this is vulgar in the extreme. The word assist is not "*selon les règles de la bonne société*," but simply, "Shall I send you some?" Now, anyone can help soup. But then there are two ways, the right and the wrong. First, then, your soup plates should be held by the servant near the tureen, and you should judge the number you have to help by the quantity of soup you have, to avoid the possibility of consuming all your soup before you have helped your guests; give one spoonful of soup to each plate, and avoid by all means slopping the soup either into the tureen or over the table cloth, or over the side of the plate, all of which are extreme vulgarities. And here we beg to say—not withstanding Brummel having said, in speaking of Someone with whom he could find no other fault, that he was a sort of fellow who would come twice to soup—that, if very good, it is not vulgar to eat twice of it; but, *au contraire*, if not good, the worst possible taste.

The next thing in order is fish. Now, of fish there are several sorts; the first of the large sorts being

Salmon, the shape of which every one knows; but few people have a whole salmon at table. The fish should be served always on a strainer, covered with a small dinner napkin, and the cook should be careful that it be sent to table whole and unbroken. It should be laid on its side, and garnished with fried smelts; it should be cut with the trowel, or fish-knife, immediately down the middle of the side, and helped from the centre to the back, one slice back and a small slice towards the belly, which is the richest and fattest part; care should be taken that the slices are not broken, and with each slice a fried smelt be given.

Cod-fish should be helped differently. Cutting from the back to the thin part, crossways, and the fish divided so as to give each person a small portion.

Mackerel, if boiled, should be divided into four; that is, place your trowel or fish-knife under the flesh at the tail, and raise up the flesh to the head, then divide the side in the middle, giving half of the side to each person, and leaving the bone and head and tail in the dish.

Herrings should be helped by giving one to each person.

Eels are always cut in small pieces, and all the attention required is that those which are the largest are the best.

Patties and Entrees ought to be so arranged that they can be served with a spoon, and require no carving. The roast is therefore the next thing that calls for observation.

A Leg of Mutton is, or rather ought to be served exactly the reverse side to a haunch of mutton; that is, it ought to lie on the flat side, and so show the beveled side to the carver. A slice is cut in the center; and then the carver is to cut to the bone right and left, the thick side being most esteemed. The best fat is that which lies at the thick end, near to the bone; there is not much of it, but it is considered a delicacy.

A Sirloin of Beef. The most elegant way to cut this joint is by making an incision from the chine-bone to the flap, directly in the center, and helping from either side. However, this is not the most economical way; and therefore it is to be cut thin on the outside, from the chine-bone to the flaps, with fat from underneath. Many people like the under side, or inner loin. If this is eaten hot—and it is best hot—the joint should be turned, and the meat cut across in slices rather thicker than from the top side. Great care should be taken not to splash the gravy in turning, by placing the fork well into the flap, so as to secure a firm hold.

A Fore Quarter of Lamb should be carved without; removing the shoulder from the dish on which it is served. This is very difficult; but if well done, very elegant. First, then, let us give all the directions necessary for this dish. When it comes before the carver, he should place the carving-knife under the shoulder, and dexterously remove it. Having so done, he should place under the shoulder a slice of fresh butter, and then prepare some salt, cayenne pepper, and the juice of an orange or a lemon, which should be also poured over the part of the lamb from which the shoulder has been separated, and then pour the gravy with the gravy-spoon over the lamb, so that the butter, etc., may amalgamate well with the gravy.

You have then the breast and the ribs, and the shoulder on the dish, ready to help your friends. Before separating the ribs, you must cut off the breast, the bones of which the butcher has previously broken, so as to enable you to do it with ease. As, however, many people cannot carve *so* much in one dish, perhaps the better plan is to place the shoulder on a separate dish, when it can be cut precisely as a shoulder of mutton, and the ribs and breast can be more easily divided and helped. Always take care that the butcher joints the meat, or no man can carve it.

A HIND QUARTER OF LAMB should be carved both as a leg and a loin, giving either part to those who prefer it.

A SADDLE OF LAMB must be carved like a saddle of mutton.

A LOIN OF LAMB should always be divided at the chine end of the bone, and helped in chops.

A HAUNCH OF VENISON OR MUTTON is the leg and part of the loin. It should be cut across, near the knuckle, and then another cut should pass down the center. The slices should be taken from the left and the right of this; those on the left, containing the most fat, are preferred by epicures. The fat and gravy must be equally distributed. These joints should always be served on a hot-water dish, or on a dish with a lamp under it, so as to keep the meat hot. Without one or other of these contrivances, no one should presume to give a haunch of venison to his friends. Before it is sent to table, the cook should pour over the haunch one wine-glassful of hot port wine.

AN EDGE-BONE OP BEEF should be placed on the dish standing on the thickest end. The carver should first cut off a slice horizontally from the end to the fat, an inch thick; but in helping, it cannot be cut too thin, giving to each person hard and soft fat. If cut thick it is hard and indigestible.

A ROUND OR BUTTOCK OF BEEF is cut like a fillet of veal; that is, a slice having been horizontally removed all round, the slices should be cut very thin and very even. To properly carve a large round of beef, a long carving-knife, such as is used in a cook-shop, is necessary.

A FILLET OF VEAL is a solid piece of meat without bone; it is therefore easily carved by anyone who possesses a sharp knife; the guard of the fork should be up, to prevent accidents. The veal should be well roasted; for if the gravy is in it, it is very unwholesome. The slices may be cut thicker than beef, and the stuffing should be found in the center, and in the flap which surrounds it.

A BREAST OF VEAL. The richest part of this is called the brisket. The knife must be put about four inches from this, and cut through it, which will separate the ribs from the brisket; serve whichever is liked.

CALF'S HEAD is a dish much esteemed here; but, as generally eaten, plainly boiled, it is tasteless, insipid, and very objectionable—while cooked *a la tortue*, as in France, nothing can be better. It should always be boned and rolled; but if served whole, it is to be cut down the center, and helped in slices from either side. A portion of the sweetbread, which generally accompanies a boiled calf's head, should be given with each portion. If the flesh about the socket of the eye be preferred, the eye itself being always taken out, the knife should be inserted into the orifice, and the meat scooped out. The palate—generally esteemed a delicacy—is situated under the head. This should be cut into small portions, so that every one may have a share.

SHOULDER OF MUTTON. The joint being placed with the knuckle toward the right hand, observe that there is an angular piece of fat next you. Having helped your company from this part, you may, perhaps, imagine that your shoulder of mutton is exhausted, and will not yield a further dividend. However, you may get from both sides of a large shoulder enough to help ten people, provided your slices are not too thick, which they should not be. The fat is to be cut from the aforesaid angular bit in slices, longways. After the right and left sides are exhausted, and the carver stopped by the knuckle on one side and the blade-bone on the other, the end of the shoulder is to be turned, and cut straight down from the center bone to the end, comprising the three best slices of the joint. If more is required, the shoulder may be reversed on the dish, and four good slices will be found on the under side.

SADDLE OF MUTTON. This best joint of the sheep is carved in several ways; the usual way is to cut from the tail to the end close to the chine-bone, taking the slices horizontally. Another plan is to cut close to the backbone, taking slices sideways, so as to help each person with a piece like a mutton chop, without the bone and very thin. Another way is to commence, not quite close to the backbone, and so cut slices, rounding them a little that they will curl on the plate, cutting in such a way that the knife slants toward the flaps or fat, and so that the top of each slice is fat and the bottom lean; and for a small party, this is by far the most elegant and the best way to carve this excellent joint.

HAM. There perhaps is no joint about which there has been so much contention as the carving of this excellent dish. For family use, do not have the skin removed, but let it be sent to table as it is dressed. Out from the thick end, where there is most fat; as a ham served hot is always eaten with veal or poultry, you can thus eat the fat. Continue cutting your ham in this way, and you will be able to eat it all; whereas, in any other way, all the lean will be eaten, and a large quantity of fat, which will become rancid, will be lost.

CARVING HAM FOR A PARTY. The best informed say, carve it like a leg of mutton, that is, beginning in the center, cut right and left in thin slices; we say, commence at the knuckle, and cut a thick slice off, and then cut thin slices as they do in the cook-shops—for, rely on it, by this time they have found out the most economical way of carving ham.

A SUCKING PIG must be divided down the middle, and decapitated. This ought to be done by the cook, and the two sides placed flat on the dish. Supposing, therefore, this to have been previously done, the carver is to take off the shoulders and the legs, and help the ribs in such pieces as he thinks convenient. The ribs are considered best, and you should give plenty of the sauce or gravy with each plate.

HARE. There are two ways of carving this difficult dish. The first is to cut close to the back-bone from the shoulder to the rump on either side, previously dividing the legs; take off the shoulders; cutting the back-bone in three or four pieces, and getting two slices on either side of the hare. The ear is considered the best part. Another way of carving a hare is by taking off the legs and shoulders, and cutting it round through the back-bone, dividing into seven or eight pieces. It is better to bone a hare.

A Rabbit is carved very differently. The legs and shoulders are to be taken off, and the back divided into three or four pieces.

Fowls when boiled have their legs bent inwards, and tucked into the belly. A fowl must never be removed from the dish and placed upon the carver's plate; nothing can be more vulgar. The wing is to be removed with a good slice of the breast, the only difficulty being to hit the joint. To effect this, the knife is to be passed between the leg and the body, and the leg turned back with the fork. The carver must commence just above where the breast turns, and cut down slanting; then begin at the rump end, and cut the breast at either side, keeping the fork in that part of the breast nearest the rump, and turning it toward the carver; the side-bones may easily be removed, the back broken in half, and the two sides are then easily taken off. All this can only be learned by practice; and although we have endeavored to describe it, we feel that it requires practice to carry out the directions.

A Pheasant is carved precisely as a fowl. It is only necessary to say that ladies like the wings and breast.

Wild Duck. This bird is only helped from the breast, which is to be first scored in such a way as afterward to form the slice. Lemon juice, cayenne, salt, and port wine made hot, should be ready to pour over it; then the previously scored slices are to be cut and helped. The breast is the only eatable part, except when hashed.

PARTRIDGE. This bird is carved precisely as a fowl. The legs and the back are the best parts; give them to the ladies, and let the rest of the company have the wings and breast.

PIGEONS are usually cut straight down the middle, and a half sent to each person.

TURKEYS are carved like geese. Never make a wing cut from the wing or pinion upward, and not from the breast downward. Give your knife a slight angle in cutting, and your slice will be larger and better.

GOOSE. To give a description of carving a goose is to say, simply, begin from the wing and cut the slices from the breast up to the breast bone, and serve each person with a slice, with some stuffing and gravy. To cut a wing or leg is vulgar in the extreme; for a large party, then, a second goose is necessary; but lest our readers should say, "That is an easy way to avoid telling us how we ought to dismember this bird," we will continue. If you wish to do a vulgar thing, and dismember a goose, put your fork into the small end of the pinion, and press it close to the body, then put in the knife and divide the joint down; to separate the leg, first put the fork into the small end of the bone, pressing it to the body, then pass your knife between the leg and the body, turn the leg back with your fork, and it will come off. It is impossible that anything but experience will teach a person how to do this expertly; but as we said before, it never should be done when served hot. It has been said frequently, that a goose is too much for one, and not enough for two. This means that the breast, which is the only eatable part of a roasted goose, is, supposing the person to eat nothing else, too much for one and not enough for two people's dinners; another reason for never cutting off or eating the legs hot, is that they make a most excellent "devil" for breakfast the next day—therefore, why destroy a dish fit for a king?

WOODCOCKS AND SNIPES. These are both carved alike—the necessary directions being: remove the sand-bag, which contains the gall: this generally protrudes; lift up the breast near the rump; spread the tail on your toast; cut the wing, leg, and part of the back, the wing being cut full, that is, with plenty of the breast attached thereto, and you have one portion with a third of the toast; serve the other side alike, with another third of the toast, and the breast and the rest of the back give to the person you esteem the least; in fact, the legs, wings, and back, as before described, are the best, and should be served together. Snipes should be cut in half, unless you have enough to give a bird to each person.

ETIQUETTE OF THE BALL AND ASSEMBLY ROOM

Dancing has been defined as a "graceful movement of the body, adjusted by art to the measures or tunes of instruments, or of voice," and again, "agreeable to the true genius of the art, dancing is the art of expressing the sentiments of the mind, or the passions, by measured steps or bounds made in cadence, by regulated motions of the figure and by graceful gestures; all performed to the sound of musical instruments or the voice."

Lord Chesterfield, in his letters to his son, says: "Dancing is, in itself, a very trifling and silly thing: but it is one of those established follies to which people of sense are sometimes obliged to conform; and then they should be able to do it well. And though I would not have you a dancer, yet, when you do dance, I would have you dance well, as I would have you do everything you do well." In another letter, he writes: "Do you mind your dancing while your dancing master is with you? As you will be often under the necessity of dancing a minuet, I would have you dance it very well. Remember that the graceful motion of the arms, the giving of your hand, and the putting off and putting on of your hat genteelly, are the material parts of a gentleman's dancing. But the greatest advantage of dancing well is, that it necessarily teaches you to present yourself, to sit, stand, and walk genteelly; all of which are of real importance to a man of fashion."

When a gentleman accompanies a lady to a ball he will at once proceed with her to the door of the ladies' dressing room, there leaving her; and then repair to the gentlemen's dressing room. In the mean time, the lady, after adjusting her toilet, will retire to the ladies' sitting-room or wait at the door of the dressing room, according as the apartments may be arranged. After the gentleman has divested himself of hat, etc., and placed the same in the care of the man having charge of the hat-room, receiving therefore a check, and after arranging his toilet, he will proceed to the ladies' sitting-room, or wait at the entrance to the ladies' dressing room for the lady whom he accompanies, and with her enter the ball-room.

The ladies' dressing room is a sacred precinct, into which no gentleman should ever presume to look; to enter it would be an outrage not to be overlooked or forgiven.

With the etiquette of a ball-room, so far as it goes, there are but few people unacquainted. Certain persons are appointed to act as floor managers, or there will be a "Master of the Ceremonies," whose office it is to see that everything be conducted in a proper manner: if you are entirely a stranger, it is to *them* you must apply for a partner, and point out (quietly) any young lady with whom you should like to dance, when, if there be no obvious inequality of position, they will present you for that purpose; should there be an objection, they will probably select Someone they consider more suitable; but do not, on any account, go to a strange lady by yourself, and request her to dance, as she will unhesitatingly "decline the honor," and think you an impertinent fellow for your presumption.

A gentleman introduced to a lady by a floor manager, or the Master of Ceremonies, should not be refused by the lady if she be not already engaged, for her refusal would be a breach of good manners: as the Master of Ceremonies is supposed to be careful to introduce only gentlemen who are unexceptionable. But a gentleman who is unqualified as a dancer should never seek an introduction.

At a private party, a gentleman may offer to dance with a lady without an introduction, but at balls the rule is differerent. The gentleman should respectfully offer his arm to the lady who consents to dance with him, and lead her to her place. At the conclusion of the set he will conduct her to a seat, offer her any attention, or converse with her. A gentleman should not dance with his wife, and not too often with the lady to whom he is engaged.

Any presentation to a lady in a public ball-room, for the mere purpose of dancing, does not entitle you to claim her acquaintance afterwards; therefore, should you meet her, at most you may lift your hat; but even that is better avoided—unless, indeed, she first bow—as neither she nor her friends can know who or *what* you are.

In inviting a lady to dance with you, the words, "Will you *honor* me with your hand for a quadrille?" or, "Shall I have the *honor* of dancing this set with you?" are more used now than "Shall I have the *pleasure?*" or, "Will you give me the *pleasure* of dancing with you?"

If she answers that she is engaged, merely request her to name the earliest dance for which she is *not* engaged, and when she will do you the honor of dancing with you.

When a young lady declines dancing with a gentleman, it is her duty to give him a reason why, although some thoughtless ones do not. No matter how frivolous it may be, it is simply an act of courtesy to offer him an excuse; while, on the other hand, no gentleman ought so far to compromise his self-respect as to take the slightest offence at seeing a lady by whom he has just been refused, dance immediately after with Someone else.

Never wait until the signal is given to take a partner, for nothing is more impolite than to invite a lady hastily, and when the dancers are already in their places; it can be allowed only when the set is incomplete.

Be very careful not to forget an engagement. It is an unpardonable breach of politeness to ask a lady to dance with you, and neglect to remind her of her promise when the time to redeem it comes.

If a friend be engaged when you request her to dance, and she promises to be your partner for the next or any of the following dances, do not neglect her when the time comes, but be in readiness to fulfill your office as her cavalier, or she may think that you have studiously slighted her, besides preventing her obliging Someone else. Even inattention and forgetfulness, by showing how little you care for a lady, form in themselves a tacit insult.

In a quadrille, or other dance, while awaiting the music, or while unengaged, a lady and gentleman should avoid long conversations, as they are apt to interfere with the progress of the dance; while, on the other hand, a gentleman should not stand like an automaton, as though he were afraid of his partner, but endeavor to render himself agreeable by those "airy nothings" which amuse for the moment, and are in harmony with the occasion.

The customary honors of a bow and curtsy should be given at the commencement and conclusion of each dance.

Lead the lady through the quadrille; do not *drag* her, nor clasp her hand as if it were made of wood, lest she, not unjustly, think you a bear.

You will not, if you are wise, stand up in a quadrille without knowing something of the figure; and if you are master of a few of the steps, *so much the better*. But dance quietly; do not kick and caper about, nor sway your body to and fro; dance only *from the hips downwards*; and lead the lady as lightly as you would tread a measure with a spirit of gossamer.

Do not pride yourself on doing the "steps neatly," unless you are ambitious of being taken for a dancing-master; between whose motions and those of a *gentleman* there is a great difference.

Unless a man has a very graceful figure, and can use it with great elegance, it is better for him to *walk* through the quadrilles, or invent some gliding movement for the occasion.

When a lady is standing in a quadrille, though not engaged in dancing, a gentleman not acquainted with her partner should not converse with her.

When an unpracticed dancer makes a mistake, we may apprise him of his error; but it would be very impolite to have the air of giving him a lesson.

Immediate attention should be paid to any request made by the Master of Ceremonies, and all misunderstandings respecting the dance should be referred to him, his decision being deemed final. Otherwise his superintendence of the ball will be attended with great inconvenience.

When forming for quadrilles, if by any oversight you should accidentally occupy another couple's place, on being informed of the intrusion, you should immediately apologize to the incommoded party, and secure another position.

Contending for a position in quadrilles, at either head or sides, indicates an irritable and quarrelsome disposition altogether unsuited for an occasion where all should meet with kindly feelings.

When a company is divided into different sets, persons should not attempt to change their places without permission from the Master of Ceremonies.

No persons engaged in a quadrille or other dance that requires their assistance to complete the set, should leave the room or sit down before the dance is finished, unless on a very urgent occasion, and not even then without previously informing the Master of Ceremonies, that he may find substitutes.

If a lady waltz with you, beware not to press her waist; you must only lightly touch it with the palm of your hand, lest you leave a disagreeable impression not only on her *ceinture*, but on her mind.

Above all, do not be prone to quarrel in a ballroom; it disturbs the harmony of the company, and should be avoided if possible. Recollect that a thousand little derelictions from strict propriety may occur through the ignorance or stupidity of the aggressor, and not from any intention to annoy; remember, also, that the *really well-bred women* will not thank you for making them conspicuous by over-officiousness in their defence, unless, indeed, there be some serious or glaring violation of decorum. In small matters, ladies are both able and willing to take care of themselves, and would prefer being allowed to overwhelm the unlucky offender in their own way.

When a gentleman has occasion to pass through an assemblage of ladies, where it is absolutely impossible to make his way without disturbing them; or when he is obliged to go in front, because he cannot get behind them, it is but common courtesy for him to express his regret at being compelled to annoy them.

A gentleman having two ladies in charge may, in the absence of friends, address a stranger, and offer him a partner, asking his name previous to an introduction, and mentioning that of the lady to him or not, as he may think proper.

It is improper to engage or reengage a lady to dance without the permission of her partner.

Never forget that ladies are to be first cared for, to have the best seats, the places of distinction, and are entitled in all cases to your courteous protection.

Young ladies should avoid sauntering through an assembly-room alone; they should either be accompanied by their guardian or a gentleman.

Neither married nor young ladies should leave a ball-room assemblage, or other party, unattended. The former should be accompanied by other married ladies, and the latter by their mother or guardian. Of course, a gentleman is a sufficient companion for either.

Young ladies should avoid attempting to take part in a dance, particularly a quadrille, unless they are familiar with the figures. Besides rendering themselves awkward and confused, they are apt to create ill-feeling, by interfering with, and annoying others. It were better for them to forego the gratification of dancing than to risk the chances of making themselves conspicuous, and the subject of animadversion. As we have elsewhere said, modesty of deportment should be the shining and preeminent characteristic of woman. She should be modest in her attire, in language, in manners, and general demeanor. Beauty becomes irresistible when allied to this lodestone of attraction; plainness of features is overlooked by it; even positive homeliness is rendered agreeable by its influence.

When a gentleman escorts a lady to a ball, he should dance with *her* first, or offer so to do; and it should be his care to see that she is provided with a partner whenever she desires to dance.

After dancing, a gentleman should invariably conduct a lady to a seat, unless she otherwise desires; and, in fact, a lady should not be unattended, at any time, in a public assembly.

When you conduct your partner to her seat, thank her for the pleasure she has conferred upon you, and do not remain too long conversing with her.

When that long and anxiously desiderated hour, the hour of supper, has arrived, you hand the lady you attend up or down to the supper-table. You remain with her while she is at the table, seeing that she has all that she desires, and then conduct her back to the dancing-rooms.

If, while walking up and down a public promenade, you should meet friends or acquaintances whom you don't intend to join, it is only necessary to salute them the first time of passing; to bow or nod to them at every round would be tiresome, and therefore improper; have no fear that they will deem you odd or unfriendly, as, if they have any sense at all, they can appreciate your reasons. If you have anything to say to them, join them at once.

We have already alluded to the necessity of discarding all cant terms and phrases from conversation, not only in assembly-rooms, but on all occasions; and we would particularly caution our young lady friends against even the recognition of those *equivoques* and *double entendre* which the other sex sometimes inconsiderately, but oftener determinedly, introduce.

Neither by smiles nor blushes should they betray any knowledge of the hidden meaning that lurks within a phrase of doubtful import, nor seem to recognize anything which they could not with propriety openly make a subject of discourse. All indelicate expressions should be to them as the Sanscrit language is to most people, incomprehensible. All wanton glances and grimaces, which are by libertines considered as but so many invitations to lewdness, should be strictly shunned.

No lady can be too fastidious in her conduct, or too guarded in her actions. A bad reputation is almost as destructive of happiness to her as absolute guilt; and of her character we may say with the poet:

A breath can make them, or a breath unmake.

In dancing, generally, the performers of both sexes should endeavor to wear a pleasant countenance; and in presenting hands, a slight inclination of the head, in the manner of a salutation, is appropriate and becoming. Dancing is certainly supposed to be an enjoyment, but the sombre countenance of some who engage in it, might almost lead to the belief that it were a solemn duty being performed. If those who laugh in church would transfer their merriment to the assembly-room, and those who are sad in the assembly-room would carry their gravity to the church, they both might discover the appositeness of Solomon's declaration, that "there is a time to be merry and a time to be sad."

We have already alluded to the importance of a correct use of language in conversation, and though we are aware that it is absolutely impossible to practice it without a certain degree of education, yet we would urge that the habit which many acquire, more through carelessness than ignorance, of disregarding it, is worthy of consideration. Many a young lady has lost a future husband by a wanton contempt for the rules of Lindley Murray.

Though hardly a case in point, we cannot forego the opportunity of recording an incident in the career of a young man "about town," who, anxious to see life in all its phases, was induced to attend a public ball, the patrons of which were characterized more for their peculiarity of manners than their extraordinary refinement. On being solicited by an acquaintance, whom he respected for his kindness of heart and integrity rather than for his mental accomplishments, to dance with his daughter, he consented, and was accordingly introduced to a very beautiful young lady. Ere the dance commenced, and while the musicians were performing the "Anvil Chorus," from "Trovatore," the young lady asked: "Do you know what that 'ere is?"

Supposing that she meant *air*, and wishing to give her an opportunity of making herself happy in the thought of imparting a valuable piece of information, in utter disregard of the principles of Mrs. Opie, he replied, "No." "Why," said she, "that's the Anvel Core-ri-ous."

With an expletive more profane than polite, he suddenly found his admiration for the lady as much diminished by her ignorance, as it had before been exalted by her beauty.

At private assemblies, it should be the effort of both ladies and gentlemen to render themselves as agreeable as possible to all parties. With this purpose in view, the latter should, therefore, avoid showing marked preferences to particular ladies, either by devoting their undivided attentions or dancing exclusively with them. Too often, the belle of the evening, with no other charms than beauty of form and feature, monopolizes the regards of a circle of admirers, while modest merit, of less personal attraction, is both overlooked and neglected. We honor the generous conduct of those, particularly the "well-favored," who bestow their attentions on ladies who, from conscious lack of beauty, least expect them.

On the other hand, no lady, however numerous the solicitations of her admirers, should consent to dance repeatedly, when, by so doing, she excludes other ladies from participating in the same amusement; still less, as we have elsewhere hinted, should she dance exclusively with the same gentleman, to the disadvantage of others.

Both ladies and gentlemen should be careful about introducing persons to each other without being first satisfied that such a course will be mutually agreeable.

The custom, in this country, particularly among gentlemen, of indiscriminate introductions, is carried to such a ridiculous extent, that it has often been made the subject of comment by foreigners, who can discover no possible advantage in being made acquainted with others with whom they are not likely to associate for three minutes, in whom they take not the slightest interest, and whom they probably will never again encounter, nor recognize if they should. Besides, every one has a right to exercise his own judgment and taste in the selection of acquaintances, and it is clearly a breach of politeness to thrust them upon your friend or associate, without knowing whether it will be agreeable to either party.

EVENING PARTIES

THE etiquette of the ball-room being disposed of, let us now enter slightly into that of an evening party.

The invitations issued and accepted for an evening party will be written in the same style as those already described for a dinner-party. They should be sent out *at least* three weeks before the day fixed for the event, and should be replied to within a week of their receipt, accepting or declining with regrets. By attending to these courtesies, the guests will have time to consider their engagements and prepare their dresses, and the hostess will also know what will be the number of her party.

A lady, invited to an evening party, may request a gentleman to accompany her, even though he may not have received an invitation from the hostess.

In most of the American cities nine o'clock is the hour which custom has established as the time for the lady to be in her parlor, ready to receive her guests, and by ten o'clock all the guests should arrive. It is an affectation, not entirely devoid of assumption and impudence, for people to purposely delay their appearance till a very late hour.

As the ladies and gentlemen arrive, each should be shown to a room exclusively provided for their reception; and the gentleman conducts the lady in his charge to the door of the ladies' dressing room, while he goes to the gentlemen's apartment, each to prepare their toilet suitably to entering the reception-room.

In the room set apart for the ladies, attendants should be in waiting to assist in uncloaking, and helping to arrange the hair and toilet of those who require it.

After completing her toilet, the lady waits at the door of her dressing room till the gentleman joins her, and they make their *entree* together.

In large and formal parties, it is generally customary for the servant to announce the names of the guests as they enter the room, but this is a ceremony well enough dispensed with, except on occasions of very large and formal parties.

It is the business of the lady of the house to be near the door to receive her guests; if she is not there, you need not go hunting through the crowd after her.

As the guests enter the room, it is not necessary for the lady of the house to advance each time toward the door, but merely to rise from her seat to receive their courtesies and congratulations. If, indeed, the hostess wishes to show particular favor to some peculiarly honored guests, she may introduce them to others, whose acquaintance she may imagine will be especially suitable and agreeable.

It is very often the practice of the gentleman of the house to introduce one gentleman to another, but occasionally the lady performs this office; when it will, of course, be polite for the persons thus introduced to take their seats together for the time being.

When entering a private ball or party, the visitor should invariably bow to the company. No well-bred person would omit this courtesy in entering a drawing-room; and although the entrance to a large assembly may be unnoticed by all present, its observance is not the less necessary. It is the thoughtless absence of good manners in large and mixed companies, where a greater degree of studied politeness is indispensable, that renders them sometimes so unpleasant.

A separate room or convenient buffet should be appropriated for refreshments, and to which the dancers may retire; and cakes and biscuits, with lemonade, handed round.

Of course a supper is provided at all private parties; and this requires, on the part of the hostess, a great deal of attention and supervision. It usually takes place between the first and second parts of the programme of the dances, of which there should be several prettily written or printed copies distributed about the room.

It will be well for the hostess, even if she be very partial to the amusement, and a graceful dancer, not to participate in it to any great extent, lest her lady guests should have occasion to complain of her monopoly of the gentlemen, and other causes of neglect.

A few dances will suffice to show her interest in the entertainment, without unduly trenching on the attention due to her guests.

The hostess or host, during the progress of a party, will courteously accost and chat with their friends, and take care that the ladies are furnished with seats, and that those who wish to dance are provided with partners. A gentle hint from the hostess, conveyed in a quiet lady-like manner, that certain ladies have remained unengaged during several dances, is sure not to be neglected by any gentleman. Thus will be studied the comfort and enjoyment of the guests, and no lady, in leaving the house, will be able to feel the chagrin and disappointment of not having been invited to "stand up" in a dance during the whole evening.

For any of the members, either sons or daughters, of the family at whose house the party is given, to dance frequently or constantly, denotes decided ill-breeding. The ladies of the house should not occupy those places in a quadrille which others may wish to fill, and they should, moreover, be at leisure to attend to the rest of the company; and the gentlemen should be entertaining the married ladies and those who do not dance.

In private parties, a lady is not to refuse the invitation of a gentleman to dance, unless she be previously engaged. The hostess must be supposed to have asked to her house only those persons whom she knows to be perfectly respectable and of unblemished character, as well as pretty equal in position; and thus, to decline the offer of any gentleman present, would be a tacit reflection on the gentleman or lady of the house.

If one lady refuses you, do not ask another who is seated near her to dance the same set. Do not go immediately to another lady, but chat a few moments with the one whom you first invited, and then join a group or gentlemen friends for a few moments, before seeking another partner.

In private parties, where dancing is the chief part of the evening's entertainment, it is not in conformity with the rules of etiquette for a young lady to dance with one gentleman repeatedly, to the exclusion of all others who may solicit her hand, even though the favored individual be her suitor. However complimentary to the lady to be the recipient of a gentleman's undivided attentions, or however gratifying it may be for him to manifest his devotion to the lady of his choice, such a course is an exhibition of selfishness which ought not to be displayed in an assemblage of ladies and gentlemen who have congregated for mutual enjoyment.

It is not considered *comme il faut* to ask a married lady to dance, when her husband is present, without previously ascertaining whether it be agreeable to him.

Gentlemen will not get together in groups to the neglect of the ladies.

The members of an invited family should never be seen conversing with each other at a party.

If you accompany your wife to a dancing party, be careful not to dance with her, except perhaps the first set.

Where there are no programmes, engagements should not be made until the dance is announced.

When the dance is over, the gentleman conducts his partner to her seat; and, unless he chooses to sit beside her, bows and withdraws.

While dancing, a lady should consider herself engaged to her partner, and therefore not at liberty to hold a flirtation, between the figures, with another gentleman; and should recollect that it is the gentleman's part to lead her, and hers to follow his directions.

In a circle, we should not pass before a lady; neither should we present anything by extending the arm over her, but pass round behind and present it. In case we cannot do it, we say, *I ask your pardon, etc.*

In ascending a staircase with ladies, go at their side or before them.

A correct ear for music does not pertain to every one, and those who are deficient in this respect should refrain from dancing. Let not the unpracticed dancer attempt quadrilles. A novice necessarily perplexes and annoys a partner. On the other hand, nowhere perhaps has a kindly disposition more pleasing opportunities of conferring small benefits than in a ball-room. Those who are expert in dancing may gently apprise the unskillful of an error, and this without giving the slightest offense, or seeming to dictate; while such as dance well, and are solicited to dance, should carefully avoid speaking of it. They ought rather to seek to contribute to less fortunate persons a full share in the evening's amusement. A lady may do this by gently hinting to a gentleman who solicits her hand for another dance, that such a lady has remained unengaged. No gentleman will neglect such a suggestion.

There is a custom which is sometimes practiced both in the assembly room and at private parties, which cannot be too strongly reprehended; we allude to the habit of ridicule and ungenerous criticism of those who are ungraceful or otherwise obnoxious to censure, which is indulged in by the thoughtless, particularly among the dancers. Of its gross impropriety and vulgarity we need hardly express an opinion; but there is such an utter disregard for the feelings of others implied in this kind of negative censorship, that we cannot forbear to warn our young readers to avoid it. The *Koran* says: "Do not mock—the mocked may be better than the mocker." Those you condemn may not have had the same advantages as yourself in acquiring grace or dignity, while they may be infinitely superior in purity of heart and mental accomplishments. The advice of Chesterfield to his son, in his commerce with society, to *do as you would be done by*, is founded on the Christian precept, and worthy of commendation. Imagine yourself the victim of another's ridicule, and you will cease to indulge in a pastime which only gains for you the hatred of those you satirize, if they chance to observe you, and the contempt of others who have noticed your violation of politeness, and abuse of true sociality.

We conclude our strictures on this subject with the following passage from the essays of Addison: "But what an absurd thing it is, to pass over all the valuable characteristics of individuals, and fix our attention on their infirmities—to observe their imperfections more than their virtues—and to make use of them for the sport of others, rather than for our own improvement."

In whatever relation with the fair sex, and under whatsoever circumstances, it is the duty—we may add, the practice—of a gentleman to so deport himself as to avoid giving any cause of offense.

In private parties, where people meet for the pleasure of conversation, remember occasionally to change your place. Opportunities will readily occur, such, for instance, as the opening of a portfolio of prints, or the showing of any article of taste or science. You will thus avoid the awkwardness of being either left alone, or constraining the master or mistress of the house to commiserate your isolated condition.

If you are asked by the lady of the house, at an evening party, to sing, and you can really do so well, comply at once; but never sing at the request of another person. If you cannot or do not choose to sing, say so at once with seriousness and gravity, and put an end to the expectation promptly. After singing once or twice, cease and give place to others.

When singing or playing is going on, if you have no taste for music, you should still be profoundly silent. To converse, is annoying to the rest of the company, rude to the mistress of the house, and cruel to the performer.

Carefully avoid all peculiarities of manner; and every wish to show off, or to absorb conversation to yourself. Be also very careful not to appear to be wiser than the company. If a fact in history is mentioned, even if it be not quite correct, do not set the narrator right, unless in a very delicate and submissive manner. If an engraving of distant scenery or foreign buildings is shown, do not industriously point out inaccuracies. It may be that such occur, but finding fault is never acceptable; it conveys a censure on the taste or information of the possessor; or it suggests that he has been imposed upon—an idea which is always productive of mortification. Such attempts to appear wiser than the rest of the company, interfere with the pleasure of the party, and the person who falls into them is never long acceptable.

People sometimes say, that they are not invited to parties; they complain of neglect, and are out of humor with the world. Let such persons consider whether they have not brought upon themselves the neglect which they deplore.

Should the guests be numerous, and the space scarcely sufficient for their accommodation, it would be considered extremely ill-bred to take a place previously engaged; or, when joining a country dance, to push in at the middle or upper end. You must take your station below the last couple who are standing up.

If there be a supper, the gentleman should conduct to the supper-room his last partner, unless he have a prior engagement, or is asked by the host to do otherwise. In the latter case, he should provide his partner with a substitute, at the same time making a handsome apology.

No gentleman should offer his services to conduct a lady home, without being acquainted with her, unless he has been requested so to do by the host.

When any of the carriages of the guests are announced, or the time for their departure arrived, they should make a slight intimation to the hostess, without, however, exciting any observation, that they are about to depart. If this cannot be done without creating too much bustle, it will be better for the visitors to retire quietly without saying good-night, for when people are seen to be leaving, it often breaks up the party. An opportunity, however, may previously be sought of intimating to the hostess your intention to retire, which is more respectful.

During the course of the week, the hostess will expect to receive from every guest a call, where it is possible, or cards expressing the gratification experienced from her entertainment. This attention is due to every lady for the pains and trouble she has been at, and tends to promote social, kindly feelings.

VISITING

NEXT in order to the ceremonials of dinner or evening parties, are customary calls, comprised under the general head of visiting. They are those of ceremony, friendship, or condolence, and occupy no small portion of time.

Such visits are necessary, in order to maintain good feeling between the members of society; they are required by the custom of the age in which we live, and must be carefully attended to.

First, then, are visits of ceremony, merging occasionally into those of friendship, but uniformly required after dining at a friend's house. Professional men are not however, in general, expected to pay such visits, because their time is preoccupied; but they form almost the only exception.

Visits of ceremony must be necessarily short. They should on no account be made before the hour, nor yet during the time of luncheon. Persons who intrude themselves at unwonted hours are never welcome; the lady of the house does not like to be disturbed when she is perhaps dining with her children; and the servants justly complain of being interrupted at the hour when they assemble for their noon-day meal. Ascertain, therefore, which you can readily do, what is the family hour for luncheon, and act accordingly.

Half an hour amply suffices for a visit of ceremony. If the visitor be a lady, she may remove her victorine, but on no account either the shawl or bonnet, even if politely requested to do so by the mistress of the house. Some trouble is necessarily required in replacing them, and this ought to be avoided. If, however, your visit of ceremony is to a particular friend, the case is different; but even then, it is best to wait till you are invited to do so; and when you rise for the purpose the lady of the house will assist you.

Favorite dogs are never welcome visitors in a drawing-room. Many people have even a dislike to such animals. They require watching, lest they should leap upon a chair or sofa, or place themselves upon a lady's dress, and attentions of this kind are much out of place. Neither ought a mother, when paying a ceremonial visit, to be accompanied by young children. It is frequently difficult to amuse them, and, if not particularly well trained at home, they naturally seize hold of books, or those ornaments with which it is fashionable to decorate a drawing-room. The lady of the house trembles for the fate of a beautiful shell, or vase, or costly book. She does not like to express her uneasiness, and yet knows not how to refrain. Therefore leave the children at home; or, if they accompany you in the carriage, let them remain till your visit is over. If you have an infant, the nurse may await your return, or be left in an ante-room, unless a decided request be made to the contrary.

If during your short visit the conversation begins to flag, it will be best to retire. The lady of the house may have some engagement at a fixed hour, and by remaining even a few minutes longer, she may be put to serious inconvenience. Do not, however, seem to notice any silent hint, by rising hastily; but take leave with quiet politeness, as if your time were fully expired. When other visitors are announced, retire as soon as possible, and yet without letting it appear that their arrival is the cause. Wait till the bustle of their entrance is over, and then rise from your chair, take leave of the hostess, and bow politely to the guests. By so doing you will save the lady of the house from being obliged to entertain two sets of visitors.

Should you call by chance at an inconvenient hour, when perhaps the lady is going out, or sitting down to luncheon, retire as soon as possible, even if politely asked to remain. You need not let it appear that you feel yourself an intruder; every well-bred or even good-tempered person knows what to say on such an occasion; but politely withdraw, with a promise to call again, if the lady seems to be really disappointed.

If your acquaintance or friend is from home, leave a card,[1] whether you call in a carriage or not. If in the latter, the servant will answer your inquiry, and receive your card; but on no account ask leave to go in and rest; neither urge your wish if you fancy that the lady whom

---

[1] When the caller is about to leave the city for a protracted absence, it is usual to put the letters P. P. C. in the left hand corner of the card; they are the initials of the French phrase, "*pour prendre congé*"—to take leave, and may with equal propriety stand for *presents parting compliments.*

you desire to see is really at home, or even if you flatter yourself that she would make an exception in your favor. Some people think that the form of words, "Not at home," is readily understood to mean that the master or mistress of the house have no wish to see even his or her most intimate friends. However this may be, take care that you do not attempt to effect an entrance.

Visits of courtesy or ceremony are uniformly paid at Christmas, or at the commencement of a new year, independently of family parties; a good old custom, the observance of which is always pleasing, and which should be carefully attended to. It is uniformly right to call on patrons, or those from whom kindness has been received.

In visiting your intimate friends, ceremony may generally be dispensed with.

Keep a strict account of your ceremonial visits. This is needful, because time passes rapidly; and take note how soon your calls are returned. You will thus be able, in most cases, to form an opinion whether or not your frequent visits are desired. Instances may however occur, when, in consequence of age or ill health, it is desirable that you should call, without any reference to your visits being returned. When desirous to act thus, remember that, if possible, nothing should interrupt the discharge of this duty.

Among relations and intimate friends, visits of mere ceremony are unnecessary. It is, however, needful to call at suitable times, and to avoid staying too long if your friend is engaged. The courtesies of society, as already noted must ever be maintained, even in the domestic circle, or among the nearest friends.

In leaving cards you must thus distribute them: one for the lady of the house and her daughters—the latter are sometimes represented by turning up the edge of the card—one for the master of the house, and if there be a grown up son or a near male relation staying in the house, one for him. But though cards are cheap, you must never have more than three at a time at the same house. As married men have, or are supposed to have, too much to do to make ceremonial calls, it is the custom for a wife to take her husband's cards with her, and to leave one or two of them with her own. If, on your inquiring for the lady of the house, the servant replies, "Mrs. So-and-so is not at home, but Miss So-and-so is," you should leave a card, because young ladies do not receive calls from gentlemen unless they are very intimate with them, or have passed the rubicon of thirty summers. It must be remembered, too, that where there is a lady of the house, your call is to her, not to her husband, except on business.

Morning calls may be divided into three heads: Those paid at the time already specified; weekly visits to intimate friends, or by young persons to those advanced in life; and monthly visits, which are generally ceremonious.

With respect to the first, be very careful that you do not acquire the character of a *day goblin*. A day goblin is one of those persons who, having plenty of leisure, and a great desire to hear themselves talk, make frequent inroads into their friends' houses. Though perhaps well acquainted with the rules of etiquette, they call at the most unreasonable hours. If the habits of the family are early, you will find them in the drawing-room at eleven o'clock. It may be they are agreeable and well-informed people; but who wishes for calls at such a strange hour! Most families have their rules and occupations. In one, the lady of the house attends to the education of her children; in another, domestic affairs engross a portion of the morning; some ladies are fond of gardening, others of music or painting. It is past endurance to have such pursuits broken in upon for the sake of a day goblin, who, having gained access, inflicts his or her presence till nearly luncheon time, and then goes off with saying, "Well, I have paid you a long visit;" or "I hope that I have not stayed too long."

A well-bred person always receives visitors at whatever time they may call, or whoever they may be; but if you are occupied and cannot afford to be interrupted by a mere ceremony, you should instruct the servant *beforehand* to say that you are "not at home." This form has often been denounced as a falsehood, but a lie is no lie unless intended to deceive; and since the words are universally understood to mean that you are engaged, it can be no harm to give such an order to a servant. But, on the other hand, if the servant once admits a visitor within the hall, you should receive him at any inconvenience to yourself. A lady should never keep a visitor waiting more than a minute, or two at the most, and if she cannot avoid doing so, must apologize on entering the drawing-room.

In good society, a visitor, unless he is a complete stranger, does not wait to be invited to sit down, but takes a seat at once easily. A gentleman should never take the principal place in the room, nor, on the other hand, sit at an inconvenient distance from the lady of the house. He must hold his hat gracefully, not put it on a chair or table, or, if he wants to use both hands, must place it on the floor close to his chair. A well-bred lady, who is receiving two or three visitors at a time, pays equal attention to all, and attempts, as much as possible, to generalize the conversation, turning to all in succession. The last arrival, however, receives a little more attention at first than the others, and the latter, to spare her embarrasment, should leave as soon as convenient. People who out-sit two or three parties of visitors, unless they have some particular motive for doing so, come under the denomination of "bores." A "bore" is a person who does not know when you have had enough of his or her company.

Be cautious how you take an intimate friend *uninvited* even to the house of those with whom you may be equally intimate, as there is always a feeling of jealousy that another should share your thoughts and feelings to the same extent as themselves, although good breeding will induce them to behave *civilly* to your friend on your account.

Ladies in the present day are allowed considerable license in paying and receiving visits; subject, however, to certain rules, which it is needful to define.

Young married ladies may visit their acquaintances alone; but they may not appear in any public places unattended by their husbands or elder ladies. This rule must never be infringed, whether as regards exhibitions, or public libraries, museums, or promenades; but a young married lady is at liberty to walk with her friends of the same age, whether married or single. Gentlemen are permitted to call on married ladies at their own houses. Such calls the usages of society permit, but never without the knowledge and full permission of husbands.

Ladies may walk unattended in the streets, being careful to pass on as becomes their station—neither with a hurried pace, nor yet affecting to move slowly. Shop-windows, in New York especially, afford great attractions; but it is by no means desirable to be seen standing before them, and most assuredly not alone. Be careful never to look back, nor to observe too narrowly the dresses of such ladies as may pass you. Should anyone venture to address you, take no heed, seem not to hear, but hasten your steps. Be careful to reach home in good time. Let nothing ever induce you to be out after dusk, or when the lamps are lighted. Nothing but unavoidable necessity can sanction such acts of impropriety.

Lastly, a lady never calls on a gentleman, unless professionally or officially. It is not only ill-bred, but positively improper to do so. At the same time, there is a certain privilege in age, which makes it possible for an old bachelor like myself to receive a visit from any married lady whom I know very intimately, but such a call would certainly not be one of ceremony, and always presupposes a desire to consult me on some point or other. I should be guilty of shameful treachery, however, if I told anyone that I had received such a visit, while I should certainly expect that my fair caller would let her husband know of it.

When morning visitors are announced, rise and advance toward them. If a lady enters, request her to be seated on a sofa; but if advanced in life, or the visitor be an elderly gentleman, insist on their accepting an easy chair, and place yourself by them. If several ladies arrive at the same time, pay due respect to age and rank, and seat them in the most honorable places; these, in winter, are beside the fire.

Supposing that a young lady occupies such a seat, and a lady older than herself, or superior in condition, enters the room, she must rise immediately, and having courteously offered her place to the new comer, take another in a different part of the room.

If a lady is engaged with her needle when a visitor arrives, she ought to discontinue her work, unless requested to do otherwise: and not even then must it be resumed, unless on very intimate terms with her acquaintance. When this, however, is the case, the hostess may herself request permission to do so. To continue working during a visit of ceremony would be extremely discourteous; and we cannot avoid hinting to our lady readers, that even when a particular friend is present for only a short time, it is somewhat inconsistent with etiquette to keep their eyes fixed on a crochet or knitting-book, apparently engaged in counting stitches, or unfolding the intricacies of a pattern. We have seen this done, and are, therefore, careful to warn them on the subject. There are many kinds of light and elegant, and even useful work, which do not require close attention, and may be profitably pursued; and such we recommend to be always on the work-table at those hours which, according to established practice, are given to social intercourse.

It is generally customary in the country to offer refreshment to morning visitors. If they come from a considerable distance, and are on intimate terms, hospitality requires that you should invite them to take luncheon. In town it is otherwise, and you are not expected to render any courtesy of the kind, except to aged or feeble persons, or to Someone who, perhaps, is in affliction, and to whom the utmost kindliness should be shown.

When your visitor is about to take leave, rise, and accompany her to the door, mindful, at the same time, that the bell is rung, in order that a servant may be in attendance. If the master of the house is present, and a lady is just going away, he must offer her his arm, and lead her to the hall or passage door. If her carriage be in waiting, he will, of course, hand her into it. These attentions are slight, and some persons may think they are scarcely worth noticing. Nevertheless, they are important, and we are the more earnest to press them on the attention of our readers, because we have witnessed the omission of such acts of courtesy in families where a very different mode of conduct might be expected.

And here, turning aside for a brief space from the subject-matter of our discourse, we desire earnestly to impress upon mothers who have sons growing up, the great importance of early imbuing them with the principles of true politeness, and consequent attention to its most trifling observances. What matters it if a tall lad pushes into a room before one of his mother's visitors; or, if he chance to see her going into church, instead of holding the door in a gentlemanly manner, he lets it swing in her face when he has himself entered; or whether he comes into the drawing-room with his hat on, unobservant of lady visitors, or lolls in an arm-chair reading the newspaper?

"What signifies it?" some will say—"why tease a youth about such matters? He will learn manners as he grows up." We think otherwise, and do not scruple to affirm, that he can never learn real gentlemanly politeness from anyone but his mother. The neglect of small courtesies in early life, and the outward or mental boorishness to which it leads, has been, to our certain knowledge, a more fruitful source of wretchedness in many homes, than we have either time or inclination to relate.

In this changing world, visits of condolence must be also occasionally paid; and concerning such, a few necessary rules may be briefly stated.

Visits of condolence should be paid within a week after the event which occasions them; but if the acquaintance be slight, immediately after the family appear at public worship. A card should be sent up; and if your friends are able to receive you, let your manners and conversation be in harmony with the character of your visit. It is courteous to send up a mourning card; and for ladies to make their calls in black silk or plain-colored apparel. It denotes that they sympathize with the afflictions of the family; and such attentions are always pleasing.

Gentlemen will do well to bear in mind that, when they pay morning calls, they must carry their hats with them into the drawing-room; but on no account put them on the chairs or table. There is a graceful manner of holding a hat, which every well-bred man understands.

When calling upon a friend who is boarding, do not go up till the servant returns with an invitation; and never enter a room without previously knocking at the door, and receiving an invitation to come in. Such observances are indispensable, even between the nearest friends.

A gentleman when calling upon a lady, and finding that one of her lady friends is with her, must rise when the visitor takes her leave, and accompany her to the hall door; or if she has a carriage, he should hand her into it—supposing, however, that no gentleman related to the mistress of the house be present. If your visit has been of sufficient length, you can take your leave when accompanying the lady out of the room.

It happens occasionally that two persons are visiting different members of the same family. When this occurs, and one visitor takes leave, the lady or gentleman whose visitor has just left should remain in the drawing-room. It is considered discourteous to do otherwise.

In most families in this country, evening calls are the most usual. Should you chance to visit a family, and find that they have a party, present yourself, and converse for a few minutes with an unembarrassed air; after which you may retire, unless urged to remain. A slight invitation, given for the sake of courtesy, ought not to be accepted. Make no apology for your unintentional intrusion; but let it be known, in the course of a few days, that you were not aware that your friends had company.

An excellent custom prevails in some families of inviting their guests for a given period. Thus, for example, an invitation is sent, stating that a friend's company is requested on a certain day, mentioning also for what length of time, and if a carriage cannot be offered to meet the visitor, stating expressly the best mode of coming and going. We recommend this admirable plan to the master and mistress of every dwelling which is sufficiently capacious to admit of receiving an occasional guest. A young lady is perhaps invited to spend a little time in the country, but she cannot possibly understand whether the invitation extends to a few days, or a week, or a month, and consequently is much puzzled with regard to the arrangement of her wardrobe. Domestic consultations are held; the letter is read over and over again; every one gives a different opinion, and when the visit is entered upon, somewhat of its pleasure is marred through the embarrassment occasioned by not knowing when to propose taking leave.

In receiving guests, your first object should be to make them feel at home. Begging them to make themselves at home is not sufficient. You should display a genuine unaffected friendliness. Whether you are mistress of a mansion or a cottage, and invite a friend to share your hospitality, you must endeavor, by every possible means, to render the visit agreeable. This should be done without apparent effort, that the visitor may feel herself to be a partaker in your home enjoyments, instead of finding that you put yourself out of the way to procure extraneous pleasures. It is right and proper that you seek to make the time pass lightly; but if, on the other hand, you let a visitor perceive that the whole tenor of your daily concerns is altered on her account, a degree of depression will be felt, and the pleasant anticipations which she most probably entertained will fail to be realized. Let your friend be assured, from your manner, that her presence is a real enjoyment to you—an incentive to recreations which otherwise would not be thought of in the common routine of life. Observe your own feelings when you happen to be the guest of a person who, though he may be very much your friend, and really glad to see you, seems not to know what to do either with you or himself; and again, when in the house of another you feel as much at ease as in your own. Mark the difference, more easily felt than described, between the manners of the two, and deduce therefrom a lesson for your own improvement.

If you have guests in your house, you are to appear to feel that they are all equal for the time, for they all have an equal claim upon your courtesies. Those of the humblest condition will receive *full as much attention* as the rest, in order that you shall not painfully make them feel their inferiority.

Always avoid the foolish practice of deprecating your own rooms, furniture, or viands, and expressing regrets that you have nothing better to offer. Neither should you go to the other extreme of extolling any particular thing or article of food. The best way is to say nothing about these matters. Neither is it proper to urge guests to eat, or to load their plates against their inclinations.

Endeavor to retain your friends as long as they like to prolong their visit. When they intimate an intention to leave you, if you really desire their continuance somewhat longer, frankly say so. Should they, however, have fixed the time, and cannot prolong their stay, facilitate their going by every means in your power; and, while you kindly invite them to renew their visit, point out to them any places of interest on the road, and furnish such information as you possess.

If invited to spend a few days at a friend's house, conform as much as possible to the habits of the family. When parting for the night, inquire respecting the breakfast hour, and ascertain at what time the family meet for prayers. If this right custom prevails, be sure to be in time; and obtain any necessary information from the servant who waits upon you. Give as little trouble as possible; and never think of apologizing for the extra trouble which your visit occasions. Such an apology implies that your friend cannot conveniently entertain you. Your own good sense and delicacy will teach you the desirability of keeping your room tidy, and your articles of dress and toilet as much in order as possible. If there is a deficiency of servants, a lady will certainly not hesitate to make her own bed and to do for herself as much as possible, and for the family all that is in her power.

We presume that few people will leave a friend's house without some expression of regret, and some acknowledgment proffered for the pleasure that has been afforded them. Instances to the contrary have come within our knowledge, and therefore we remind our youthful readers especially, that this small act of politeness is indispensable, not in the form of a set speech, but by a natural flowing forth of right feeling. It is also proper, on returning home, to inform your friends of your safe arrival; the sense which you entertain of their hospitality, and the gratification derived from your visit, may be also gracefully alluded to.

The chain which binds society together is formed of innumerable links. Let it be your part to keep those links uniformly bright; and to see that neither dust nor rust accumulate upon them.

STREET ETIQUETTE

THE books of etiquette tell you, that if you have been introduced to a lady and you afterward meet her in the street, you must not bow to her unless she bow first, in order, as the books say, that she may have an opportunity to cut you if she does not wish to continue the acquaintance. This is the English fashion. But on the continent of Europe the rule is reversed, and no lady, however intimate you may be with her, will acknowledge you in the street unless you first honor her with a bow of recognition. But the American fashion is not like either of them. For here the really well-bred man always politely and respectfully bows to every lady he knows, and, if she is a well-bred woman, she acknowledges the respect paid her. If she expects no further acquaintance, her bow is a mere formal, but *always respectful*, recognition of the good manners which have been shown her, and no gentleman ever takes advantage of such politeness to push a further acquaintance uninvited. But why should a lady and gentleman, who know who each other are, scornfully and doggedly pass each other in the streets as though they were enemies? There is no good reason for such *impoliteness*, in the practice of politeness. As compared with the English, the French or continental fashion is certainly more consonant with the rules of good breeding. But the American rule is better than either, for it is based upon the acknowledged general principle, that it is every gentleman's and lady's duty to be polite in all places. Unless parties have done something to forfeit the respect dictated by the common rules of politeness, there should be no deviation from this practice. It is a ridiculous idea that we are to practice ill-manners in the name of etiquette.

While walking the street no one should be so absent-minded as to neglect to recognize his friends. If you do not stop, you should always bow, touch your hat, or bid your friend good day. If you stop, you can offer your hand without removing your glove. If you stop to talk, retire on one side of the walk. If your friend has a stranger with him and you have anything to say, you should apologize to the stranger. Never leave your friend abruptly to see another person without asking him to excuse your departure. If you meet a gentleman of your acquaintance walking with a lady whom you do not know, lift your hat as you salute them. If you know the lady, you should salute her first.

Never *nod* to a lady in the street, neither be satisfied with touching your hat, *but take it off*—it is a courtesy her sex demands.

A gentleman should never omit a punctilious observance of the rules of politeness to his recognized acquaintances, from an apprehension that he will not be met with reciprocal marks of respect. For instance, he should not refuse to raise his hat to an acquaintance who is accompanied by a lady, lest her escort should, from ignorance or stolidity, return his polite salutation with a nod of the head. It is better not to see him, than to set the example of a rude and indecorous salutation. In all such cases, and in all cases, he who is most courteous has the advantage, and should never feel that he has made a humiliating sacrifice of his personal dignity. It is for the party whose behavior has been boorish to have a consciousness of inferiority.

A gentleman meeting a lady acquaintance on the street, should not presume to join her in her walk without ascertaining that his company would be entirely agreeable. It might be otherwise, and she should frankly say so. A married lady usually leans upon the arm of her husband; but single ladies do not, in the day, take the arm of a gentleman, unless they are willing to acknowledge an engagement. Gentlemen always give place to ladies, and gentlemen accompanying ladies, in crossing the street.

If you have anything to say to a lady whom you may happen to meet in the street, however intimate you may be, do not stop her, but turn round and walk in company; you can take leave at the end of the street.

When you are passing in the street, and see coming toward you a person of your acquaintance, whether a lady or an elderly person, you should offer them the wall, that is to say, the side next the houses. If a carriage should happen to stop in such a manner as to leave only a narrow passage between it and the houses, beware of elbowing and rudely crowding the passengers, with a view to get by more expeditiously; wait your turn, and if any of the persons before mentioned come up, you should edge up to the wall, in order to give them the place. They also as they pass, should bow politely to you.

If stormy weather has made it necessary to lay a plank across the gutters, which has become suddenly filled with water, it is not proper to crowd before another, in order to pass over the frail bridge.

In walking with a lady, it is customary to give her the right arm; but where circumstances render it more convenient to give her the left, it may properly be done. If you are walking with a lady on a crowded street like Broadway, by all means give her the outside, as that will prevent her from being perpetually jostled and run against by the hurrying crowd.

You should offer your arm to a lady with whom you are walking whenever her safety, comfort, or convenience may seem to require such attention on your part. At night your arm should always be tendered, and also when ascending the steps of a public building. In walking with any person you should keep step with military precision, and with ladies and elderly people you should always accommodate your speed to theirs.

If a lady with whom you are walking receives the salute of a person who is a stranger to you, you should return it, not for yourself, but for her.

When a lady whom you accompany wishes to enter a store, you should hold the door open and allow her to enter first, if practicable; for you must never pass before a lady anywhere, if you can avoid it, or without an apology.

In England, it is a mark of low breeding to smoke in the streets. But in America the rule does not hold to quite that extent; though, even here, it is not often that you catch "a gentleman of the strictest sect," in the street with a cigar or pipe in his mouth. For a man to go into the street with a lady on his arm and a cigar in his mouth is a shocking sight, which no gentleman will ever be guilty of exhibiting; for he inevitably subjects the woman to the very worst of suspicions.

Avoid the disgusting habit of spitting.

No gentleman will stand in the doors of hotels, nor on the corners of the streets, gazing impertinently at the ladies as they pass. That is such an unmistakable sign of a loafer, that one can hardly imagine a well-bred man doing such a thing.

Never offer to shake hands with a lady in the street if you have on dark gloves, as you may soil her white ones. If you meet a lady friend with whom you wish to converse, you must not stop, but turn and walk along with her; and should she be walking with a gentleman, first assure yourself that you are not intruding before you attempt to join the two in their walk.

After twilight, a young lady would not be conducting herself in a becoming manner, by walking alone; and if she passes the evening with anyone, she ought, beforehand, to provide Someone to come for her at a stated hour; but if this is not practicable, she should politely ask of the person whom she is visiting, to permit a servant to accompany her. But, however much this may be considered proper, and consequently an obligation, a married lady, well educated, will disregard it if circumstances prevent her being able, without trouble, to find a conductor.

If the host wishes to accompany you himself, you must excuse yourself politely for giving him so much trouble, but finish, however, by accepting. On arriving at your house, you should offer him your thanks. In order to avoid these two inconveniences, it will be well to request your husband, or Someone of your relatives, to come and wait upon you; you will, in this way, avoid all inconveniences, and be entirely free from that harsh criticism which is sometimes indulged in, especially in small towns, concerning even the most innocent acts.

If, when on your way to fulfill an engagement, a friend stops you in the street, you may, without committing any breach of etiquette, tell him of your appointment, and release yourself from a long talk, but do so in a courteous manner, expressing regret for the necessity.

In inquiring for goods at a shop or store, do not say, I want so and so, but say to the shopman—Show me such or such an article, if you please—or use some other polite form of address. If you are obliged to examine a number of articles before you are suited, apologize to the shopkeeper for the trouble you give him. If, after all, you cannot suit yourself, renew your apologies when you go away. If you make only small purchases, say to him—I am sorry for having troubled you for so trifling a thing.

You need not stop to pull off your glove to shake hands with a lady or gentleman. If it is warm weather it is more agreeable to both parties that the glove should be on—especially if it is a lady with whom you shake hands, as the perspiration of your bare hand would be very likely to soil her glove.

If a lady addresses an inquiry to a gentleman on the street, he will lift his hat, or at least touch it respectfully, as he replies. If he cannot give the information required, he will express his regrets.

When tripping over the pavement, a lady should gracefully raise her dress a little above her ankle. With her right hand she should hold together the folds of her gown and draw them toward the right side. To raise the dress on both sides, and with both hands, is vulgar. This ungraceful practice can be tolerated only for a moment when the mud is very deep.

Most American ladies in our cities wear too rich and expensive dresses in the street. Some, indeed, will sweep the side-walks with costly stuffs only fit for a drawing-room *or* a carriage. This is in bad taste, and is what ill-natured people would term snobbish.

TRAVELING

As a general rule, travelers are selfish. They pay little attention either to the comforts or distresses of their fellow-travelers; and the commonest observances of politeness are often sadly neglected by them. In the scramble for tickets, for seats, for state-rooms, or for places at a public table, the courtesies of life seem to be trampled under foot. Even the ladies are sometimes rudely treated and shamefully neglected in the headlong rush for desirable seats in the railway cars. To see the behavior of American people on their travels, one would suppose that we were anything but a refined nation; and I have often wondered whether a majority of our travelers could really make a decent appearance in social society.

When you are traveling, it is no excuse that because others outrage decency and propriety you should follow their example, and fight them with their own weapons. A rush and scramble at the railway ticket office is always unnecessary. The cars will not leave until every passenger is aboard, and if you have ladies with you, you can easily secure your seats and afterward procure the tickets at leisure. But suppose you do lose a favorite seat by your moderation! Is it not better to suffer a little inconvenience than to show yourself decidedly vulgar? Go to the cars half an hour before they start, and you will avoid all trouble of this kind.

When seated, or about to seat yourself in the cars, never allow considerations of personal comfort or convenience to cause you to disregard the rights of fellow-travelers, or forget the respectful courtesy due to woman. The pleasantest or most comfortable seats belong to the ladies, and you should never refuse to resign such seats to them with a cheerful politeness. Sometimes a gentleman will go through a car and choose his seat, and afterward vacate it to procure his ticket, leaving his overcoat or carpet bag to show that the seat is taken. Always respect this token, and never seize upon a seat thus secured, without leave, even though you may want it for a lady. It is not always necessary for a gentleman to rise after he has seated himself and offer his seat to a lady, particularly if the lady is accompanied by another gentleman; for there may still be eligible vacant seats in the cars. But should you see a lady come alone, and if the seats in the car all appear to be filled, do not hesitate to offer her yours, if you have no ladies in your company. And should a lady motion to seat herself beside you, rise at once and offer her the choice of the two seats. These are but common courtesies that every well-bred man will at all times cheerfully offer to the other sex.

Making acquaintances in the cars, although correct enough, is a measure of which travelers generally appear to be very shy. There is no reason for this, as acquaintances thus picked up need never be recognized again unless you please. If a stranger speaks to you, always answer him politely, and if his conversation proves disagreeable, you have no alternative but to change your seat.

In steamers do not make a rush for the supper table, or make a glutton of yourself when you get there. Never fail to offer your seat on deck to a lady, if the seats all appear to be occupied, and always meet half way any fellow-passenger who wishes to enter into conversation with you. Some travelers are so exclusive that they consider it a presumption on the part of a stranger to address them; but such people are generally foolish, and of no account. Sociable intercourse while traveling is one of its main attractions. Who would care about sitting and moping for a dozen of hours on board a steamer without exchanging a word with anybody? and this must be the fate of the exclusives when they travel alone. Even ladies, who run greater risks in forming steamboat acquaintances than the men, are allowed the greatest privileges in that respect. It might not be exactly correct for a lady to make a speaking acquaintance of a gentleman; but she may address or question him for the time being without impropriety.

Fellow-passengers, whether on a steamboat or in the cars, should at all times be sociable and obliging to one another. Those who are the reverse of this may be set down either as selfish, foolish, or conceited.

In the cars you have no right to keep a window open for your accommodation, if the current of air thus produced annoys or endangers the health of another. There are a sufficient number of discomforts in traveling, at best, and it should be the aim of each passenger to lessen them as much as possible, and to cheerfully bear his own part. Life is a journey, and we are all fellow-travelers.

If in riding in an omnibus, or crossing a ferry with a friend, he wishes to pay for you, never insist upon paying for yourself or for both. If he is before you, let the matter pass without remark.

MARRIAGE

In speaking of marriage, it is not merely with reference to its social importance, but as regards certain observances, concerning which no work on Etiquette has yet given any explicit rules.

First, then, with respect to the preliminary subject of courtship. That unseen monitor, who has already suggested many points for consideration to lady readers, would now say to them: Before you admit the attentions of a gentleman who wishes to pay you his addresses, very carefully examine your respective tastes and dispositions; and settle in your own mind what are the most important requisites of happiness in a married state. With this view, you must enter upon the consideration of the subject with a calm and decisive spirit, which will enable you to see where your true happiness lies, and to pursue it with determined resolution. In matters of business, follow the advice of such as are able to guide you; and as regards the subject of marriage, turn not away from the counsel of those who are appointed to watch over and direct you.

If a gentleman gives you reason to believe that he wishes to engage your affections, seek the advice of your parents, that they may gain for you every necessary particular with regard to his morals and disposition, and means of suitably providing for you. If, unhappily, death has deprived you of parents, ask counsel of Someone who will care for you, and on whose friendship you can rely. Remember that you have little knowledge of the world, and that your judgment has not arrived at full maturity. But however circumstanced, avoid, as you would the plague, any attentions from a gentleman whose moral character renders him undeserving your regard.

Let neither rank nor fortune, nor the finest order of intellect, nor yet the most winning manners, induce you to accept the addresses of an irreligious man. You dare not ask the blessing of your Heavenly Father upon such addresses; and without His blessing, what happiness can you expect? Men often say, "that whatever their own opinions may be, they will marry religious women." This may be; but woe to a religious woman, if she allows herself to be thus beguiled! Supposing your admirer be a sensible man, he will like religion in you for his own sake; if, on the contrary, such is not the case, and you become his wife, he will often, though perhaps without intention, distress you by his remarks; and in either case, if you have children, you will suffer much in seeing that your endeavors to form their minds to virtue and piety, and to secure their present and eternal happiness, are regarded with indifference, or at least that you are not assisted in your efforts.

Remember, also, that no happiness can be expected in the marriage state, unless the husband be worthy of respect. Do not marry a weak man; he is often intractable or capricious, and seldom listens to the voice of reason; and most painful must it be to any sensible woman to have to blush for her husband, and feel uneasy every time he opens his lips. Still worse, if it should please God to give her children, if she cannot point to the example of their father as leading to what is excellent and of good report; nor yet to his precepts and instructions as their rule of conduct. One thing is certain, that a weak man uniformly shows his consequence by contradicting his wife, because he will not have it supposed that he is under her influence.

Advances, or offers of marriage, are made in a thousand different ways; but, however tendered, receive them courteously, and with dignity. If a letter comes to you, answer it as becomes a gentlewoman—your own heart will dictate what you ought to say. Questions have arisen with regard to the wording of such letters, but no certain rule can be laid down; whether it be answered in the first or third person, must depend upon the degree of acquaintance which has previously existed. No young lady would certainly head her letter with— "Dear Sir," to a suitor whom she scarcely knows, or to one whom she intends refusing. She ought, however, on no account, either to receive or answer letters of the kind without showing them to her mother; or, if unfortunately without parents, she will do well to consult some judicious female friend.

Never trifle with the affections of a man who loves you; nor admit of marked attentions from one whose affection you cannot return. Some young ladies pride themselves upon the conquests which they make, and would not scruple to sacrifice the happiness of an estimable person to their reprehensible vanity. Let this be far from you. If you see clearly that you have become an object of especial regard to a gentleman, and do not wish to encourage his addresses, treat him honorably and humanely, as you hope to be used with generosity by the person who may engage your own heart. Do not let him linger in suspense, but take the earliest opportunity of carefully making known your feelings on the subject. This may be done in a variety of ways. A refined ease of manner will satisfy him, if he has any discernment, that his addresses will not be acceptable. Should your natural disposition render this difficult, show that you wish to avoid his company, and he will presently withdraw; but if even this is difficult—and who can lay down rules for another?—allow an opportunity for explanation to occur. You can then give him a polite and decisive answer; and be assured that, in whatever manner you convey your sentiments to him, if he be a man of delicacy and right feeling, he will trouble you no further. Let it never be said of you, that you permit the attentions of an honorable man when you have no heart to give him; or that you have trifled with the affections of one whom you perhaps esteem, although you resolve never to marry him. It may be that his preference gratifies, and his conversation interests you; that you are flattered by the attentions of a man whom some of your companions admire; and that, in truth, you hardly know your own mind on the subject. This will not excuse you. Every young woman ought to know the state of her own heart; and yet the happiness and future prospects of many an excellent man have been sacrificed by such unprincipled conduct.

Remember that if a gentleman makes you an offer, you have no right to speak of it. If you possess either generosity or gratitude for offered affection, you will not betray a secret which does not belong to you. It is sufficiently painful to be refused, without incurring the additional mortification of being pointed out as a rejected lover.

If, on the contrary, you encourage the addresses of a deserving man, behave honorably and sensibly. Do not lead him about as if in triumph, nor take advantage of the ascendency which you have gained by playing with his feelings. Do not seek for occasions to tease him, that you may try his temper; neither affect indifference, nor provoke lovers' quarrels, for the foolish pleasure of reconciliation. On your conduct during courtship will very much depend the estimation in which you will be held by your husband in after life.

Assuming that the important day is fixed, and that the bidden guests have accepted the invitations, a few observations may be useful, especially to those who live retired in the country.

The bride uniformly goes to church in the same carriage with her parents, or with those who stand in their place; as, for instance, if the father is deceased, an elder brother or uncle, or even guardian, accompanies her mother and herself. If, unhappily, she is an orphan, and has no relations, a middle-aged lady and gentleman, friends of her parents, should be requested to take their place. A bridesmaid will also occupy a seat in the same carriage.

The bridegroom finds his way to church in a separate carriage with his friends, and he will show his gallantry by handing the bride from her carriage, and paying every attention to those who accompany her. Any omission in this respect cannot be too carefully avoided.

When arrived at the altar, the father of the bride, or, in default of such relation, the nearest connection, or some old friend, gives away the bride. The bridesmaids stand near the bride; and either her sister, or some favorite friend, will hold the gloves or handkerchief, as may be required, when she ungloves her hand for the wedding ring. When the ceremony is completed, and the names of the bride and bridegroom are signed in the vestry, they first leave the church together, occupying by themselves the carriage that waits to convey them to the house of the bride's father and mother, or that of the guardian, or friend, by whom the bridal breakfast is provided.

The wedding cake uniformly occupies the center of the table. It is often tastefully surrounded with flowers, among which those of the fragrant orange ought to be conspicuous. After being cut according to the usages observed on such occasions, the oldest friend of the family proposes the lady's health; that of the bridegroom is generally proposed by some friend of his own, if present; but if this is not the case, by his father-in-law, or any of his new relatives, who will deem it incumbent upon them to say something gratifying to him while proposing his health, which courtesy he must acknowledge as best he can. After this the bride withdraws, in order to prepare for leaving the parental roof, by taking off her wedding, and putting on her traveling dress; although it happens not unfrequently that the bride remains in another apartment, and thus avoids the fatigue and embarrassment of appearing at the breakfast table. When this occurs, her place beside the bridegroom must be occupied by a near relation or friend. But whether present, or remaining apart with a few friends, all who are invited to do honor to the bride must appear in full dress. Bracelets may be worn on one or both wrists. Black of any kind is wholly inadmissible; not even black satin can be allowed; and widows must attire themselves either in quiet colored suits, or else in silver gray.

On such festive occasions, all appear in their best attire, and assume their best manners. Peculiarities that pertain to past days, or have been unwarily adopted, should be guarded against; mysteries concerning knives, forks, and plates, or throwing "an old shoe" after the bride, are highly reprehensible, and have long been exploded. Such practices may seem immaterial, but they are not so. Stranger guests often meet at a wedding breakfast; and the good breeding of the family may be somewhat compromised by neglect in small things.

If the lady appears at breakfast, which is certainly desirable, she occupies, with her husband, the center of the table, and sits by his side—her father and mother taking the top and bottom, and showing all honor to their guests. When the cake has been cut, and every one is helped—when, too, the health of the bride and bride-groom has been drunk, and every compliment and kind wish has been duly proffered and acknowledged—the bride, attended by her friends, withdraws; and when ready for her departure the newly-married couple start off on their wedding journey, generally about two or three o'clock, and the rest of the company shortly afterward take their leave.

In some circles it is customary to send cards almost immediately to friends and relations, mentioning at what time and hour the newly-married couple expect to be called upon. Some little inconvenience occasionally attends this custom, as young people may wish to extend their wedding tour beyond the time first mentioned, or, if they go abroad, delays may unavoidably occur. It is therefore better to post-pone sending cards, for a short time at least.

Fashions change continually with regard to wedding-cards. A few years since they were highly orna-mented, and fantastically tied together; now silver-edged cards are fashionable; but, unquestionably, the plainer and more unostentatious a wedding-card, the more lady-like and becoming it will be.

No one to whom a wedding-card has not been sent ought to call upon a newly-married couple.

When the days named for seeing company arrive, remember to be punctual. Call, if possible, the first day, but neither before nor after the appointed hour. Wedding-cake and wine are handed round, of which every one partakes, and each expresses some kindly wish for the happiness of the newly-married couple.

Taking possession of their home by young people is always a joyous period. The depressing influence of a wedding breakfast, where often the hearts of many are sad, is not felt, and every one looks forward to years of prosperity and happiness.

If the gentleman is in a profession, and it happens that he cannot await the arrival of such as call, according to invitation on the wedding-card, an apology must be made, and, if possible, an old friend of the family should represent him. A bride must on no account receive her visitors without a mother, or sister, or some friend being present, not even if her husband is at home. This is imperative. To do otherwise is to disregard the usages of society. We remember once calling on a very young bride, and found her alone. Conjectures were made by every visitor with regard to such a strange occurrence, and their surprise was still more increased, when it became known that the young lady returned her calls equally unattended.

Wedding visits must be returned during the course of a few days, and parties are generally made for the newly-married couple, which they are expected to return. This does not, however, necessarily entail much visiting; neither is it expected from young people, whose resources may be somewhat limited, or when the husband has to make his way in the world.

DOMESTIC ETIQUETTE AND DUTIES

"The little community to which I gave laws," said the Vicar of Wakefield, "was regulated in the following manner—We all assembled early, and after we had saluted each other with proper ceremony, (for I always thought fit to keep up some mechanical forms of good breeding, without which, freedom ever destroys friendship,) we all knelt in gratitude to that Being who gave us another day. So also when we parted for the night."

We earnestly recommend that the precepts and example of the good old Vicar should be followed and adopted by every newly-married couple. With regard to the first, the courtesies of society should never be omitted, in even the most trivial matters; and, as respects the second, what blessing can be reasonably expected to descend upon a house wherein the voice of thanksgiving is never heard, nor yet protection sought by its acknowledged head!

On the wife especially devolves the privilege and pleasure of rendering home happy. We shall, therefore, speak of such duties and observances as pertain to her.

When a young wife first settles in her home, many excellent persons, with more zeal, it may be, than discretion, immediately propose that she should devote some of her leisure time to charitable purposes: such, for instance, as clothing societies for the poor, or schools, or district visiting. We say with all earnestness to our young friend, engage in nothing of the kind, however laudable, without previously consulting your husband, and obtaining his full concurrence. Carefully avoid, also, being induced by any specious arguments to attend evening lectures, unless he accompanies you. Remember that your Heavenly Father, who has given you a home to dwell in, requires from you a right performance of its duties. Win your husband, by all gentle appliances, to love religion; but do not, for the sake even of a privilege and a blessing, leave him to spend his evenings alone. Look often on your marriage ring, and remember the sacred vows taken by you when the ring was given; such thoughts will go far toward allaying many of these petty vexations which circumstances call forth.

Never let your husband have cause to complain that you are more agreeable abroad than at home; nor permit him to see in you an object of admiration, as respects your dress and manners, when in company, while you are negligent of both in the domestic circle. Many an unhappy marriage has been occasioned by neglect in these particulars. Nothing can be more senseless than the conduct of a young woman, who seeks to be admired in general society for her politeness and engaging manners, or skill in music, when, at the same time, she makes no effort to render her home attractive; and yet that home, whether a palace or a cottage, is the very center of her being—the nucleus around which her affections should revolve, and beyond which she has comparatively small concern.

Beware of entrusting any individual whatever with small annoyances, or misunderstandings, between your husband and yourself, if they unhappily occur. Confidants are dangerous persons, and many seek to obtain an ascendency in families by gaining the good opinion of young married women. Be on your guard, and reject every overture that may lead to undesirable intimacy. Should anyone presume to offer you advice with regard to your husband, or seek to lessen him by insinuations, shun that person as you would a serpent. Many a happy home has been rendered desolate by exciting coolness or suspicion, or by endeavors to gain importance in an artful and insidious manner.

In all money matters, act openly and honorably. Keep your accounts with the most scrupulous exactness, and let your husband see that you take an honest pride in rightly appropriating the money which he entrusts to you. "My husband works hard for every dollar that he earns," said a young married lady, the wife of a professional man, to a friend who found her busily employed in sewing buttons on her husband's coat, "and it seems to me worse than cruel to layout a dime unnecessarily." Be very careful, also, that you do not spend more than can be afforded in dress; and be satisfied with such carpets and curtains in your drawing-room as befit a moderate fortune, or professional income. Natural ornaments, and flowers tastefully arranged, give an air of elegance to a room in which the furniture is far from costly; and books judicioulsy placed, uniformly produce a good effect. A sensible woman will always seek to ornament her home, and to render it attractive, more especially as this is the taste of the present day. The power of association is very great; light, and air, and elegance, are important in their effects. No wife acts wisely who permits her sitting-room to look dull in the eyes of him whom she ought especially to please, and with whom she has to pass her days.

In middle life, instances frequently occur of concealment with regard to money concerns; thus, for instance, a wife wishes to possess an article of dress which is too costly for immediate purchase, or a piece of furniture liable to the same objection. She accordingly makes an agreement with a seller, and there are many who call regularly at houses when the husband is absent on business, and who receive whatever the mistress of the house can spare from her expenses. A book is kept by the seller, in which payments are entered; but a duplicate is never retained by the wife, and therefore she has no check whatever. We have known an article of dress paid for in this manner, far above its value, and have heard a poor young woman, who has been thus duped, say to a lady, who remonstrated with her: "Alas! what can I do? I dare not tell my husband." It may be that the same system, though differing according to circumstances, is pursued in a superior class of life. We have reason to think that it is so, and therefore affectionately warn our younger sisters to beware of making purchases that require concealment. Be content with such things as you can honorably afford, and such as your husbands approve. You can then wear them with every feeling of self-satisfaction.

Before dismissing this part of our subject, we beseech you to avoid all bickerings. What does it signify where a picture hangs, or whether a rose or a pink looks best on the drawing-room table? There is something inexpressibly endearing in small concessions, in gracefully giving up a favorite opinion, or in yielding to the will of another; and equally painful is the reverse. The mightiest rivers have their source in streams; the bitterest domestic misery has often arisen from some trifling difference of opinion. If, by chance, you marry a man of a hasty temper, great discretion is required. Much willingness, too, and prayer for strength to rule your own spirit are necessary. Three instances occur to us, in which, ladies have knowingly married men of exceeding violent tempers, and yet have lived happily. The secret of their happiness consisted in possessing a perfect command over themselves, and in seeking, by every possible means, to prevent their husbands from committing themselves in their presence.

Lastly, remember your standing as a lady, and never approve a mean action, nor speak an unrefined word; let all your conduct be such as an honorable and right-minded man may look for in his wife, and the mother of his children. The slightest duplicity destroys confidence.

The least want of refinement in conversation, or in the selection of books, lowers a woman, aye, and for ever! Follow these few simple precepts, and they shall prove to you of more worth than rubies; neglect them, and you will know what sorrow is. They apply to every class of society, in every place where man has fixed his dwelling; and to the woman who duly observes them may be given the beautiful commendation of Solomon, when recording the words which the mother of King Lemuel taught him:

The heart of her husband doth safely trust in her; she will do him good, and not evil, all the days of her life. Strength and honor are her clothing; and she shall rejoice in time to come. Her children rise up, and call her blessed; her husband also, and he praiseth her. —Prov. xxxi

We shall now address ourselves exclusively to our brethren; to them who have taken upon themselves the sacred and comprehensive names of husband and of master, who have formed homes to dwell in, and have placed therein, as their companions through life's pilgrimage, gentle and confiding ones, who have left for them all that was heretofore most dear, and whom they have sworn to love and to cherish.

When a man marries, it is understood that all former acquaintanceship *ends,* unless he intimate a desire to renew it, by sending you his own and his wife's card, if near, or by letter, if distant. If this be neglected, be sure no further intercourse it desired.

In the first place, a bachelor is seldom *very particular* in the choice of his companions. So long as he is amused, he will associate freely enough with those whose morals and habits would point them out as highly dangerous persons to introduce into the sanctity of domestic life.

Secondly, a married man has the tastes of *another* to consult; and the friend of the *husband* may not be equally acceptable to the *wife*.

Besides, newly-married people may wish to limit the circle of their friends, from praiseworthy motives of economy. When a man first *"sets up"* in the world, the burden of an extensive and indiscriminate acquaintance may be felt in various ways. Many have had cause to regret the weakness of mind which allowed them to plunge into a vortex of gaiety and expense they could ill afford, from which they have found it difficult to extricate themselves, and the effects of which have proved a serious evil to them in after-life.

Remember that you have now, as a married man, a very different standing in society from the one which you previously held, and that the happiness of another is committed to your charge. Render, therefore, your home happy by kindness and attention to your wife, and carefully watch over your words and actions. If small disputes arise, and your wife has not sufficient good sense to yield her opinion; nay, if she even seems determined to have her own way, and that tenaciously, do not get angry; rather be silent, and let the matter rest. An opportunity will soon occur of speaking affectionately, yet decidedly, on the subject, and much good will be effected. Master your own temper, and you will soon master your wife's; study her happiness without yielding to any caprices, and you will have no reason to regret yourself-control.

Never let your wife go to church alone on Sunday. You can hardly do a worse thing as regards her good opinion of you, and the well-being of your household. It is a pitiable sight to see a young wife going toward the church-door unattended, alone in the midst of a crowd, with her thoughts dwelling, it may be very sadly, on the time when you were proud to walk beside her. Remember that the condition of a young bride is often a very solitary one; and that for your sake she has left her parents' roof, and the companionship of her brothers and sisters. If you are a professional man, your wife may have to live in the neighborhood of a large city, where she scarcely knows anyone, and without those agreeable domestic occupations, or young associates, among whom she had grown up. Her garden and poultry-yard are hers no longer, and the day passes without the light of any smile but yours. You go off, most probably after breakfast, to your business or profession, and do not return till a late dinner; perhaps even not then, if you are much occupied, or have to keep up professional connections. It seems unmanly, certainly most unkind, to let your young wife go to church on Sunday without you, for the common-place satisfaction of lounging at home. To act in this manner is certainly a breach of domestic etiquette. Sunday is the only day in which you can enable her to forget her father's house, and the pleasant associations of her girlhood days—in which you can pay her those attentions which prevent all painful comparisons as regards the past. Sunday is a day of rest, wisely and mercifully appointed to loose the bonds by which men are held to the world; let it be spent by you as becomes the head of a family. Let no temptation ever induce you to wish your wife to relinquish attending Divine service, merely that she may "idle at home with you." Religion is her safeguard amid the trials or temptations of this world. And woe may be to you if you seek to withdraw her from its protection!

Much perplexity in the marriage state often arises from want of candor. Men conceal their affairs, and expect their wives to act with great economy, without assigning any reason why such should be the case; but the husband ought frankly to tell his wife the real amount of his income; for, unless this is done, she cannot properly regulate her expenses. They ought then to consult together as to the sum that can be afforded for housekeeping, which should be rather below than above the mark. When this is arranged he will find it advantageous to give into her hands, either weekly, monthly, or quarterly, the sum that is appropriated for daily expenditure, and above all things to avoid interfering without absolute necessity. The home departmemt belongs exclusively to the wife; the province of the husband is to rule the house—hers to regulate its internal movements. True it is, that some inexperienced young creatures know but little of household concerns. If this occur, have patience, and do not become pettish or ill-humored. If too much money is laid out at first, give advice, kindly and firmly, and the young wife will soon learn how to perform her new duties.

No good ever yet resulted, or ever will result from unnecessary interference. If a man unhappily marries an incorrigible simpleton, or spendthrift, he cannot help himself. Such, however, is rarely the case. Let a man preserve his own position, and assist his wife to do the same; all things will then move together, well and harmoniously.

Much sorrow, and many heart-burnings, may be avoided by judicious conduct in the outset of life, husbands should give their wives all confidence. They have entrusted to them their happiness, and should never suspect them of desiring to waste their money. Whenever a disposition is manifested to do right, express your approbation. Be pleased with trifles, and commend efforts to excel on every fitting occasion. If your wife is diffident, encourage her, and avoid seeing small mistakes. It is unreasonable to add to the embarrassments of her new condition, by ridiculing her deficiencies. Forbear extolling the previous management of your mother or your sisters. Many a wife has been alienated from her husband's family, and many an affectionate heart has been deeply wounded by such injudicious conduct; and, as a sensible woman will always pay especial attention to the relations of her husband, and entertain them with affectionate politeness, the husband on his part should always cordially receive and duly attend to her relations. The reverse of this, on either side, is often productive of unpleasant feelings.

Lastly, we recommend every young married man, who wishes to render his home happy, to consider his wife as the light of his domestic circle, and to permit no clouds, however small, to obscure the region in which she presides. Most women are naturally amiable, gentle, and complying; and if a wife becomes perverse, and indifferent to her home, it is generally her husband's fault. He may have neglected her happiness; but nevertheless it is unwise in her to retort, and, instead of faithfully reflecting the brightness that still may shine upon her, to give back the dusky and cheerless hue which saddens her existence. Be not selfish, but complying, in small things. If your wife dislikes cigars—and few young women like to have their clothes tainted by tobacco—leave off smoking; for it is, at best, an ungentlemanly and dirty habit. If your wife asks you to read to her, do not put your feet upon a chair and go to sleep. If she is fond of music, accompany her as you were wont when you sought her for a bride. The husband may say that he is tired, and does not like music, or reading aloud. This may occasionally be true, and no amiable woman will ever desire her husband to do what would really weary him. We, however, recommend a young man to practice somewhat of self-denial, and to remember that no one acts with a due regard to his own happiness who lays aside, when married, those gratifying attentions which he was ever ready to pay the lady of his love; or those rational sources of home enjoyment which made her look forward with a bounding heart to become his companion through life.

Etiquette is a comprehensive term; and its observances are nowhere more to be desired than in the domestic circle.

ON GENERAL SOCIETY

To cultivate the art of pleasing is not only worthy of our ambition, but it is the dictate of humanity to render ourselves as agreeable as possible to those around us. While, therefore, we condemn that false system of philosophy which recommends the practice of flattery and deception for the purpose of winning the regard of those with whom we come in contact, we would rather urge the sincere and open conduct which is founded on moral principle, and which looks to the happiness of others, not through any sordid and selfish aim, but for the reward which virtuous actions bestow. Indeed, we do not discover the necessity of duplicity and hypocrisy in our intercourse with society. The virtues and the graces are not antagonistic. The sacrifice of personal convenience for the accommodation of others; the repression of our egotism and self-esteem; the occasional endurance of whatever is disagreeable or irksome to us through consideration for the infirmities of others, are not only some of the characteristics of true politeness, but are in the very spirit of benevolence, and, we might add, religion.

The English have a rule of etiquette, that if you are introduced to a person of higher position in society than yourself, you must never recognize him when you meet, until you see whether he intends to notice you. The meaning of this rule is, that you should be polite to nobody until you see whether they mean to be polite to you, which is simply refusing politeness in the name of politeness itself. There is a story of an unfortunate clerk of the Treasury, who dined one day at the Beef-steak Club, where he sat next to a duke, who conversed freely with him at dinner. The next day, meeting the duke in the street, he saluted him. But his grace, drawing himself up, said: "May I know, sir, to whom I have the honor of speaking?" "Why, we dined together at the club yesterday—I am Mr. Timms, of the Treasury," was the reply. "Then," said the duke, turning on his heel, "Mr. Timms, of the Treasury, I wish you *a good morning.*" Though this anecdote is related in the English books as an example of etiquette, it is undoubtedly true that Mr. Timms, of the Treasury, was the politest man of the two; for even if he had made a mistake in being a little familiar in his politeness, had the duke been really a polite man he would have made the best of it, by returning the salutation, instead of the brutal mortification which he heaped upon the clerk of the Treasury. Everybody has read the anecdote of Washington, who politely returned the salutation of a negro, which caused his friend to ask if he "bowed to a negro." "To be sure I do; do you think that I would allow a negro to outdo me in politeness?" said Washington. This is the American rule. Everybody in this country may be polite to everybody—and if anyone is too haughty and too ill-bred to return the salutation, with him alone rests the responsibility and the shame.

A lady in company should never exhibit any anxiety to sing or play; but if she intends to do so, she should not affect to refuse when asked, but obligingly accede at once. If you cannot sing, or do not choose to, say so with seriousness and gravity, and put an end to the expectation promptly. After singing once or twice, cease and give place to others. There is an old saying, that a singer can with the greatest difficulty be set agoing, and when agoing, cannot be stopped.

Never commend a lady's musical skill to another lady who herself plays.

Modern Chesterfields, who pretend to be superlatively well-bred, tell one never to be "in a hurry." "To be in a hurry," say they, "is ill-bred." The *dictum* is absurd. It is sometimes necessary to be hurried. In the streets of the city one must hasten with the multitude. To walk or lounge, as people who have nothing else to do, in Wall Street, or Broadway, would be out of place and absurd. Judgment requires us, not less than manners, to conform slightly with the behavior of those with whom we associate or are forced to remain.

Never lose your temper at cards, and particularly avoid the exhibition of anxiety or vexation at want of success. If you are playing whist, not only keep your temper, but hold your tongue; any intimation to your partner is decidedly ungentlemanly.

Do not take upon yourself to do the honors in another man's house, nor constitute yourself master of the ceremonies, as you will thereby offend the host and hostess.

Do not press before a lady at a theater or a concert. Always yield to her, if practicable, your seat and place. Do not sit when she is standing, without offering her your place. Consult not only your own ease, but also the comfort of those around you.

Do not cross a room in an anxious manner, and force your way up to a lady merely to receive a bow, as by so doing you attract the eyes of the company toward her. If you are desirous of being noticed by anyone in particular, put yourself in their way as if by accident, and do not let them *see* that you have sought them out; unless, indeed, there be something very important to communicate.

Gentlemen who attend ladies to the opera, to concerts, to lectures, etc., should take off their hats on entering the room, and while showing them their seats. Having taken your seats remain quietly in them, and avoid, unless absolute necessity requires it, incommoding others by crowding out and in before them. If obliged to do this, politely apologize for the trouble you cause them. To talk during the performance is an act of rudeness and injustice. You thus proclaim your own ill-breeding and invade the rights of others, who have paid for the privilege of hearing the performers, and not for listening to you.

If you are in attendance upon a lady at any opera, concert, or lecture, you should retain your seat at her side; but if you have no lady with you, and have taken a desirable seat, you should, if need be, cheerfully relinquish it in favor of a lady, for one less eligible.

To the opera, or theater, ladies should wear opera hoods, which are to be taken off on entering. In this country, custom permits the wearing of bonnets; but as they are neither convenient nor comfortable, ladies should dispense with their use whenever they can.

Gloves should be worn by ladies in church, and in places of public amusement. Do not take them off to shake hands. Great care should be taken that they are well made and fit neatly.

If you would have your children grow up beloved and respected by their elders as well as their contemporaries, teach them good manners in their childhood. The young sovereign should first learn to obey, that he may be the better fitted to command in his turn.

Show, but do not show off, your children to strangers. Recollect, in the matter of children, how many are born every hour, each one almost as remarkable as yours in the eyes of its papa and mamma.

Notwithstanding that good general breeding is easy of attainment, and is, in fact, attained by most people, yet we may enlarge upon a saying of Emerson's, by declaring that the world has never yet seen "a perfect gentleman."

It is not deemed polite and respectful to smoke in the presence of ladies, even though they are amiable enough to permit it. A gentleman, therefore, is not in the habit of smoking in the parlor, for if there is nobody present to object, it leaves a smell in the room which the wife has good reason to be mortified at, if discovered by her guests.

It is very common to see persons eat, drink, and smoke to excess. Such habits are vulgar in the lowest degree. Some men pride themselves on their abilities in drinking and smoking—more especially in the latter. These are blunders that need no reasoning to expose them. The man who exhibits a tendency to excesses will, sooner or later, be shunned by all except a few of his own stamp, and not even by them be respected. Guard against excess in all things, as neither gentlemanly nor human.

Spitting is a filthy habit, and annoys one in almost every quarter, indoors and out. Since vulgarity has had its way so extensively amongst us, every youth begins to smoke and spit before he has well cut his teeth. Smoking is unquestionably so great a pleasure to those accustomed to it, that it must not be condemned, yet the spitting associated with it detracts very much from the enjoyment. No refined person will spit where ladies are present, or in any public promenade; the habit is digusting in the extreme, and one would almost wish that it could be checked in public by means of law.

Never scratch your head, pick your teeth, clean your nails, or, worse than all, pick your nose in company; all these things are disgusting.

To indulge in ridicule, whether the subject be present or absent, is to descend below the level of gentlemanly propriety. Your skill may excite laughter, but will not ensure respect.

A reverential regard for religious observances, and religious opinions, is a distinguishing trait of a refined mind. Whatever your opinions on the subject, you are not to intrude them on others, perhaps to the shaking of their faith and happiness. Religious topics should be avoided in conversation, except where all are prepared to concur in a respectful treatment of the subject. In mixed societies the subject should never be introduced.

Frequent consultation of the watch or time-pieces is impolite, either when at home or abroad. If at home, it appears as if you were tired of your company and wished them to be gone; if abroad, as if the hours dragged heavily, and you were calculating how soon you would be released.

Never read in company. A gentleman or lady may, however, look over a book of engravings with propriety.

The simpler, and the more easy and uncon-strained your manners, the more you will impress people of your good breeding. *Affectation* is one of the brazen marks of vulgarity.

It is very unbecoming to exhibit petulance, or angry feeling, though it is indulged in so largely in almost every circle. The true gentleman does not suffer his coun-tenance to be easily ruffled; and we only look paltry when we suffer temper to hurry us into ill-judged expressions of feeling. "He that is soon angry dealeth foolishly."

Commands should never be given in a command-ing tone. A gentleman requests, he does not command. We are not to assume so much importance, whatever our station, as to give orders in the "imperative mood," nor are we ever justified in thrusting the consciousness of servitude on anyone. The blunder of commanding sternly is most frequently committed by those who have themselves but just escaped servitude, and we should not exhibit to others a weakness so unbecoming.

It is a great thing to be able to *walk like a gentleman*—that is, to get rid of the awkward, lounging, swinging gait of a clown, and stop before you reach the affected and flippant step of a dandy. In short, nothing but *being a gentleman* can ever give you the air and step of one. A man who has a shallow or an impudent brain will be quite sure to show it in his heels, in spite of all that rules of manners can do for him.

A gentleman never sits in the house with his hat on in the presence of ladies for a single moment. Indeed, so strong is the force of habit, that a gentleman will quite unconsciously remove his hat on entering a parlor, or drawing-room, even if there is no one present but himself. People who sit in the house with their hats on are to be suspected of having spent the most of their time in barrooms, and similar places. *A gentleman never sits with his hat on in the theater.* Gentlemen do not generally sit even in an eating-room with their hats on, if there is any convenient place to put them.

The books on etiquette will tell you, that on waiting on a lady into a carriage, or the box of a theater, you are to take off your hat; but such *is not* the custom among polite people in this country. The inconvenience of such a rule is a good reason against its observance in a country where the practice of politeness has in it nothing of the servility which is often attached to it in countries where the code of etiquette is dictated by the courts of monarchy. In handing a lady into a carriage, a gentleman *may* need to employ both his hands, and he has no third hand to hold on to his hat.

Cleanliness of person is a distinguishing trait of every well-bred person; and this not on state occasions only, but at all times, even at home. It is a folly to sit by the fire in a slovenly state, consoling oneself with the remark, "Nobody will call call today." Should somebody call we are in no plight to receive them, and otherwise it is an injury to the character to allow slovenly habits to control us even when we are unseen.

Chesterfield inveighs against holding a man by the button, "for if people are not willing to hear you, you had much better hold your tongue than them." Button-holing is not a common vice, but pointing, nudging, hitting a man in the side with your fist, or giving him a kick of recognition under the table, are too common not to be noticed here as terrible breaches of deportment. Significant looks and gestures are equally objectionable, and must be avoided by all who desire to soar above positive vulgarity. I have often been annoyed by hearing a friend discourse on some person's failings or excellences, the person referred to being only known to the speaker. It is a bad rule *to* talk of persons at all, but more especially if the person spoken of is not known to all the listeners.

Do not offer a person the chair from which you have just risen, unless there be no other in the room.

Never take the chair usually occupied by the lady or gentleman of the house, even though they be absent, nor use the snuff-box of another, unless he offer it.

Do not lean your head against the wall. You will either soil the paper, or get your hair well powdered with lime.

Do not touch any of the ornaments in the houses where you visit; they are meant only for the use of the lady of the house, and may be admired, but not touched.

Lord Chesterfield, in his "Advice to his Son," justly characterizes an absent man as unfit for business or conversation. Absence of mind is usually affected, and springs in most cases from a desire to be thought abstracted in profound contemplations. The world, however, gives a man no credit for vast ideas who exhibits absence when he should be attentive, even to trifles. The world is right in this, and I would implore every studious youth to forget that he is studious when he enters company. I have seen many a man, who would have made a bright character otherwise, affect a foolish reserve, remove himself as far from others as possible, and in a mixed assembly, where social prattle or sincere conversation enlivened the hearts of the company, sit by himself abstracted in a book. It is foolish, and, what is worse for the absentee, it looks so. A hint on this subject is sufficient, and we do hint, that abstractedness of manner should never be exhibited; the greatest geniuses have ever been attentive to trifles when it so behooved them.

Affectation of superiority galls the feelings of those to whom it is offered. In company with an inferior, never let him feel his inferiority. An employer, who invites his confidential clerk to his house, should treat him in every way the same as his most distinguished guest. No reference to business should be made, and anything in the shape of command avoided. It is very easy by a look, a word, the mode of reception, or otherwise, to advertise to the other guests, "This is my clerk," or, "The person I now treat as a guest was yesterday laboring in my service;" but such a thing would lower the host more than it would annoy the guest. Before Burns had arrived at his high popularity, he was once invited by some puffed-up lairds to dine, in order that they might have the gratification of hearing the poet sing one of his own songs. Burns was shown into the servants' hall, and left to dine with the menials. After dinner he was invited to the drawing-room, and a glass of wine being handed to him, requested to sing one of his own songs. He immediately gave his entertainers that thrilling assertion of independence, "A man's a man for a' that," and left the moment he had finished, his heart embittered at patronage offered in a manner so insulting to his poverty.

People who have risen in the world are too apt to suppose they render themselves of consequence *in proportion to the pride they display*, and their want of attention toward those with whom they come in contact. This is a terrible mistake, as every ill-bred act recoils with triple violence against its perpetrators, by leading the offended parties to analyze them, and to question their right of assuming a superiority to which they are but rarely entitled.

Punctuality is one of the characteristics of polite-ness. He who does not keep his appointments promptly is unfit for the society of gentlemen, and will soon find himself shut out from it.

In private, watch your thoughts; in your family, watch your temper; in society, watch your tongue.

Avoid restlessness in company, lest you make the whole party as fidgety as yourself. "Do not beat the 'Devil's tattoo' by drumming with your fingers on the table; it cannot fail to annoy every one within hearing, and is the index of a vacant mind. Neither read the newspaper in an audible whisper, as it disturbs the attention of those near you. Both these bad habits are particularly offensive where most common, that is, in a counting or newsroom. Remember, that a carelessness as to what may incommode others is the sure sign of a coarse and ordinary mind; indeed, the essential part of good breeding is more in the avoidance of whatever may be disagreeable to others, than even an accurate observance of the customs of good society."

Good sense must, in many cases, determine good breeding; because the same thing that would be civil at one time and to one person, may be quite otherwise at another time and to another person.

Chesterfield says, "As learning, honor, and virtue are absolutely necessary to gain you the esteem and admiration of mankind, politeness and good breeding are equally necessary to make you welcome and agreeable in conversation and common life. Great talents, such as honor, virtue, learning, and parts, are above the generality of the world, who neither possess them themselves nor judge of them rightly in others; but all people are judges of the lesser talents, such as civility, affability, and an obliging, agreeable address and manner; because they feel the good effects of them, as making society easy and pleasing."

If you are in a public room, as a library or reading-room, avoid loud conversation or laughing, which may disturb others. At the opera, or a concert, be profoundly silent during the performances; if you do not wish to hear the music, you have no right to interfere with the enjoyment of others.

In accompanying ladies to any public place, as to a concert or lecture, you should precede them in entering the room, and procure seats for them.

Never allow a lady to get a chair for herself, ring a bell, pick up a handkerchief or glove she may have dropped, or, in short, perform any service for herself which you can perform for her, when you are in the room. By extending such courtesies to your mother, sisters, or other members of your family, they become habitual, and are thus more gracefully performed when abroad.

Etiquette in church is entirely out of place; but we may here observe that a conversation wantonly profligate always offends against good manners, nor can an irreligious man ever achieve that bearing which constitutes the true gentleman. He may be very polished and observant of form, and even if so, he will, out of respect for others, refrain from intruding his opinions and abstain from attacking those of others.

Chesterfield says, "Civility is particularly due to all women; and, remember, that no provocation whatsoever can justify any man in not being civil to every woman; and the greatest man would justly be reckoned a brute if he were not civil to the meanest woman. It is due to their sex, and is the only protection they have against the superior strength of ours; nay, even a little is allowable with women; and a man may, without weakness, tell a woman she is either handsomer or wiser than she is."

Keep your engagements. Nothing is ruder than to make an engagement, be it of business or pleasure, and break it. If your memory is not sufficiently retentive to keep all the engagements you make stored within it, carry a little memorandum book and enter them there. Especially keep any appointment made with a lady, for, depend upon it, the fair sex forgive any other fault in good breeding, sooner than a broken engagement.

The right of privacy is sacred, and should always be respected. It is exceedingly improper to enter a private room anywhere without knocking. No relation, however intimate, will justify an abrupt intrusion upon a private apartment. So the trunks, boxes, packets, papers, and letters of every individual, locked or unlocked, sealed or unsealed, are sacred. It is ill-manners even to open a book-case, or to read a written paper lying open, without permission expressed or implied. Books in an open case or on a center-table, cards in a card-case, and newspapers, are presumed to be open for examination. Be careful where you go, what you read, and what you handle, particularly in private apartments.

Avoid intermeddling with the affairs of others. This is a most common fault. A number of people seldom meet but they begin discussing the affairs of Someone who is absent. This is not only uncharitable but positively unjust. It is equivalent to trying a *cause in the absence of the person implicated*. Even in the criminal code a prisoner is presumed to be innocent until he is found guilty. Society, however, is less just, and passes judgment without hearing the defence. Depend upon it, as a certain rule, *that the people who unite with you in discussing the affairs of others will proceed to scandalize you the moment that you depart.*

Be well read also, for the sake of the general company and the ladies, in the literature of the day. You will thereby enlarge the regions of pleasurable talk. Besides, it is often necessary. Haslitt, who had entertained an unfounded prejudice against Dickens's works when they were first written, confesses that he was at last obliged to read them, because he could not enter a mixed company without hearing them admired and quoted.

Always conform your conduct, as near as possible, to the company with whom you are associated. If you should be thrown among people who are vulgar, it is better to humor them than to set yourself up, then and there, for a model of politeness. It is related of a certain king that on a particular occasion he turned his tea into his saucer, contrary to the etiquette of society, because two country ladies, whose hospitalities he was enjoying, did so. That king was a gentleman; and this anecdote serves to illustrate an important principle: namely, that true politeness and genuine good manners often not only permit, but absolutely demand, a violation of some of the arbitrary rules of etiquette. Bear this fact in mind.

Although these remarks will not be sufficient in themselves to *make* you a *gentleman*, yet they will enable you to avoid any glaring impropriety, and do much to render you easy and confident in society.

Gentility is neither in birth, manner, nor fashion—but in *the* MIND. A high sense of honor—a determination never to take a mean advantage of another—an adherence to truth, delicacy, and politeness toward those with whom you may have dealings—are the essential and distinguishing characteristics of A GENTLEMAN.